~≫~ HOPPIN' JOHN'S ~≪~
CHARLESTON, BEAUFORT & SAVANNAH

HOPPIN' JOHN'S
CHARLESTON, BEAUFORT & SAVANNAH
DINING AT HOME IN THE LOWCOUNTRY

JOHN MARTIN TAYLOR

PHOTOGRAPHS BY KELLY BUGDEN
WITH ADDITIONAL PHOTOGRAPHS BY THE AUTHOR

CLARKSON POTTER/PUBLISHERS
NEW YORK

FRONTISPIECE:
**The dining room
of the Conrad
Aiken House in
Savannah.**
RIGHT: **Clara is a
Boykin Spaniel
puppy, the state
dog of South
Carolina.**
OVERLEAF:
Forsythia.

Photographs pages 4, 10–11, 12–13, 16 (bottom), 18–19, 29, 65, 74 (bottom), 75 (top), 79, 80, 105 (bottom), 118–119, 124, 137 (center right), 141 (top), 143, 157 (top), 160–161, 164, 176 copyright © 1997 by John Martin Taylor.

Ushant by Conrad Aiken. Copyright © 1971. Reprinted by permission of Oxford University Press, Inc.

The words *Hoppin' John's* and the depiction of a chef carrying a tray of books are the trademark of John Martin Taylor, registered in the U.S. Patent and Trademark Office.

Copyright © 1997 by John Taylor
Photographs copyright © 1997 by Kelly Bugden

Published by Clarkson Potter/Publishers, 201 East 50th Street, New York, New York 10022. Member of the Crown Publishing Group.

Random House, Inc. New York, Toronto, London, Sydney, Auckland
http://www.randomhouse.com/

CLARKSON N. POTTER, POTTER, and colophon are trademarks of Clarkson N. Potter, Inc.

Printed in China

Library of Congress Cataloging-in-Publication Data
Taylor, John Martin
Hoppin' John's Charleston, Beaufort & Savannah/John Martin Taylor. Includes index.
1. Cookery. American—Southern style. 2. Cookery—South Carolina—Charleston.
3. Cookery—South Carolina—Beaufort. 4.Cookery—South Carolina—Savannah. I. Title.
TX715.2.S68T3897   1997
641.59757—dc21   96-49044

ISBN 0-517-70387-4
10 9 8 7 6 5 4 3 2 1
First Edition

DESIGN BY DONNA AGAJANIAN WITH STEPHEN FAY

FOR MIKEL

Contents

ACKNOWLEDGMENTS 8

THE LOWCOUNTRY 10

Charleston 15

THREE O'CLOCK DINNER AT THE JOHN BLAKE HOUSE 20

HUNT BREAKFAST AT HALIDON HILL 28

SOUP IN THE KITCHEN OF THE BENJAMIN PHILLIPS HOUSE 37

SUNDAY DINNER AT THE VINCENT LE SEIGNEUR HOUSE 46

SPRING DINNER AT THE WILLIAM GIBBES HOUSE 52

Beaufort 61

FROGMORE STEW AT TOMBEE PLANTATION 66

AUTUMN DINNER AT TABBY MANSE 80

BURGUNDY TASTING AND CANDLELIGHT DINNER AT THE
ELIZABETH BARNWELL GOUGH HOUSE 88

EASTER SUNDAY AT RIVERVIEW 98

LUNCH ON THE VERANDA OF THE SECESSION HOUSE 108

Savannah 117

LATE SUMMER DINNER ON ARDSLEY PARK 122

SPRING LUNCHEON AT THE JOHN STODDARD HOUSE 130

FALL LUNCHEON AT THE CONRAD AIKEN HOUSE 139

EARLY SUPPER AT THE ADAM SHORT HOUSE 150

GRILLED FISH ON A DOCK AT ISLE OF HOPE 159

CONDIMENTS 169

SOURCES 173

INDEX 174

Acknowledgments

I MINED THE BRAINS OF nearly everyone I know for this book. Fueled by a newfound patience and stability afforded me by the settling influence of my partner, Mikel Herrington, I am lucky to be able to work at home. My sister, Sue Highfield, joyously runs my business, with no help from me. My heartfelt thanks. Lee Bailey's work continues to inspire me; further, I cherish his friendship. It was he who introduced me to Roy Finamore, my dear friend and editor at Clarkson Potter, where the work has always been professional and fun. Roy allowed me to work with one of my closest friends, Kelly Bugden, whose beautiful photography captures all that the lowcountry can be. Thanks to Van Wifvat, too. I would also like to thank Lenny Allen, Amy Boorstein, Jane Treuhaft, Lauren Shakely, Robin Strashun, Joy Sikorski, and Sean Yule at Potter, and Donna Agajanian for the beautiful design.

Fran McCullough released me from contractual agreements at Bantam to work on this project. She has been a wonderful editor and friend for years. Thanks to her and my agent, Doe Coover, I have a healthy career.

To assemble a book that peeks into private homes, you must look at a lot of houses and weigh the dozens of opinions about whose is "best," all the while wondering how on earth do you choose. So many people helped me come to the decisions as they opened their minds, hearts, and the doors to their homes. I am humbled by the generosity shown me, particularly in Beaufort and Savannah, where I was a stranger. I never would have gained entry into many of the homes without the introductions provided me by friends—and friends of friends. I would like to thank everyone for the suggestions.

Some people helped in ways that can't even be explained. I doubt that the book would ever have gotten off the ground without the encouragement of my dear friend Bessie Hanahan. Debbie Marlowe (with wine recommendations) and Dana Downs (with a full glass) are always there for me, and Sara Jenkins shared cooking ideas that found their way into this collection. Dixie and Rentz Woodruff are the best in-laws anyone could hope for; their farm provided an incredible respite many times while I worked on this book.

A very special thanks to Kathy Coburn, who helped with flowers and food on two shoots; to Jennifer Hirsch, who gave up her apartment in Beaufort to two strangers; and to the gardeners Frances Parker and Patty McGee, who always welcome me into their yards with open arms.

Julia and Bob Christian provided me with an introduction to most of the people I know in Savannah; naturally, their friends were lovely and the houses they recommended, beautiful. Scot Hinson also found fabulous houses; he carried equipment, picked wildflowers, washed dishes, and fed and housed Kelly and me innumerable times in Savannah. His impressions of Savannah are very much a part of this book. In Beaufort, Will Balk and Chris Stanley, fellow booksellers at Bay Street Trading Company, introduced me to nearly everyone in town. Thank you all.

The staffs at both Rich Steele and Photo Express were always courteous, and we easily trusted our work to them. Dan Wall at Crosby's Seafood; Tony Barwick at Palmetto Pigeon Plant; Ben Cramer at LowCountry Exotic Mushroom Farm; Jack and Andrea Limehouse at Limehouse Produce; Louise Bennett, Sidi Limehouse, and Carl Witter at Rosebank Farms; and Benjamin Jenkins provided me with beautiful produce and flowers. We are lucky to have such wonderful vendors in the lowcountry.

The people who really need to be thanked, though, are the following, who opened their lovely houses to me and allowed me to make myself at home. This book is really yours.

In Charleston: Dianne and John Avlon, Dick and Vereen Coen, Susanne Leath, Charles and Celeste Patrick, Tommy and Paula Adams, Anna Crawford, Sharon Densmore, Catherine Diehl, Charles Duell, Laura Hewitt, Betsy and Buddy Jenrette, Joyce and Lowery King, Townie and Lenny Krawcheck, Avram and Jane Kronsberg, Lynn Letson, Monique Pace, Penny

RIGHT:
A statuette,
*Défense du
Sol,* on an
oysterwood
chest.

Patton, Susu Ravenel, Mary Slack, and Jock and Barbara Stender. Thanks also to Lucille Grant, Liz Young, Christopher Rose, Cheri Yates, Mary Ann and Bubba Foy, the Max Hill family, Rodney Mooneyham, and Delores Rivers.

In Beaufort: Colin and Jane Bruce Brooker, Melba Dixon, Sandy and Lin Johnson, Felicity and Jerold Panas, Connie and George Trask, Helen and Brantley Harvey, Wyatt and Sally Pringle, Lane and Anwyl Bates, and the

Lees. Also, thanks to Larry Outlaw, Flora Trask, Celia Strong, Mary Jo Valentine and Richard Brown of Sweet Temptations, and Robert Gay of Gay Fish Company.

In Savannah: Jim Cox and Ron Melander, Helen and Ned Downing, Furlow Gatewood and John Rosselli, Annie Gay, Gail Knopf, Will Quaile, Emmy and Billy Winburn, Terry Pindar, Anita Raskin, Julie Timms, and Betty Williams. Also, thanks to Myra Fields and Leola Fletcher, Damon Fowler, and Mike Sullivan.

The Lowcountry

THE LOW-LYING COASTAL PLAIN along the South Carolina–Georgia coast is protected on the ocean side by the Sea Islands, one hundred natural barriers surrounded by salt marsh. The shoreline of sandy beaches is sprinkled with sea oats, palmettos, and ancient live oaks. To leeward, creeks and estuaries meander through one of the most complicated systems of wetlands in the world. The marsh envelops the land, and into its grasses come the shrimp, crab, oysters, clams, and fishes that have characterized the local cooking since long before the English settled Charleston in the late seventeenth century.

ABOVE: **A hammock hangs from a palmetto and live oak on Edisto Island.**
RIGHT: **Oceanfront view on Folly Beach.**

The lowcountry is a subtropical world where courtyard bananas may bear fruit or be killed by winter's frost. The coastal plain extends inland about eighty miles, but the real lowcountry is the land of the rice plantations that built the fortunes and the cities of Charleston, Beaufort, and Savannah. Charleston and Beaufort were carved out of Carolina, the vast expanse of land south of Virginia that was given to the Lords Proprietors who had restored Charles II to the throne. The cities were designed as aristocratic enclaves for those with ties to the throne. Rice planters and merchants defined the economy and the character of the two towns.

Slaves from the West African rice-growing countries were imported by the thousands, and it was their hands that carved the canals and dikes out of the subtropical jungle. By 1708, there was a black majority. It was also their hands that flavored the evolving lowcountry cooking that melds country English and French traditions with the local seafood and game and the abundance of produce. Many planters and slaves lived first in the Caribbean, whence came the mahogany for the increasingly aristocratic tastes. A truly creole cuisine developed, incorporating the tropical palate of Cubans (a four-day voyage from Charleston) with the hot peppers and tomatoes—New World tastes—that Africans along the spice and slave routes had long loved.

Savannah, the most Georgian of towns, was

ABOVE: **Looking out over old rice fields at Middleburg Plantation.** RIGHT: **Vacation cottages and old plantation houses share the land on barrier islands.**

founded by a military man as a buffer between the older Carolina and Spain's Florida. Fifty years after Charleston and one hundred miles south, Georgia was settled as new territory for the crown. Savannah remained thoroughly entrenched in the customs and styles of England throughout the Georgian era. As Charleston languished after the Civil War, Savannah thrived with Victorian exuberance, tapping its vast reserves of phosphate, timber,

and naval stores, as well as cotton from the smaller farmers who had not been affected by the abolition of slavery.

The lowcountry had lent itself well to the planting of rice. With several acres of wetland for every inhabitant even today, the harnessing of the necessary waters, though a task for hundreds of slaves, was easily surmounted by

ever-changing tide, to the existential majesty of the live oak and the low plaintive calls of the shorebirds.

There has always been dichotomy in the lowcountry: the simple plantation house inland, above the saltwater line in the river, was owned by the same person who built a magnificent, showy home in town; the engineering marvels of the rice plantation were the result of the heinous institution of slavery; the very proper, mannered lifestyle in the city contradicts the earnest simplicity of hunting, fishing, and beachcombing. Traditionally, there has been little middle ground. Either you dined in Georgian grandeur or you peeled your own shrimp. You fished or you shopped. You entertained or you served.

Life in the lowcountry is every bit the fantasy that these dinners invite. These are meals served in historical context, from sideboards made locally two hundred years ago. But look closely at what's being served—fried catfish, mustard greens, and simple cakes and pies. Shrimp pulled from the local waters and relishes made with last fall's fruits. And always, beans and rice. This balance of the high and the low is perhaps what most distinguishes the lowcountry. To walk from the Adamesque drawing room onto a simple porch outfitted with comfortable modern chairs. To hunt in the briar-filled woods and still dress up for dinner.

the wealthy planters. Midway between Charleston and Savannah, Beaufort lies in the midst of one of the most valuable and pristine wetlands in the country, the ACE Basin: 350,000 acres of tidewater land bounded by the Indian-named Ashepoo, Combahee (pronounced CUMbee), and Edisto Rivers and fiercely protected by the plantation heirs. Nearly everyone is drawn outdoors here, to these waters and to the endless marsh and its

CHARLESTON

GOOD KING CHARLES II KNIGHTED his restorers, giving them all of the land south of Virginia. Carolina would be settled in his name, and in the subtropical virgin forest that covered the landscape, a miniature London—Charles Town—would be re-created to celebrate the Restoration. Founded in 1670, Charleston, as it came to be known, could not have entered the world at a more exciting time. On the heels of the scientific and intellectual developments of the seventeenth century, the city matured in the Enlightenment. With a proprietary government designed by the philosopher John Locke, the city evolved a distinctive social order based on land ownership that was its birthright; it remains its heritage.

The land, as watery as it is, predestined much of the city's charm. Built on a narrow peninsula between the Ashley and Cooper Rivers, the city looks out onto the harbor that has written its history in trade for three hundred years. Marshland surrounds the numerous barrier islands that border the city. As the city grew, those marshes were filled in to make way for the new planters and merchants, thriving in the booming rice industry.

All along the banks of the lowcountry rivers they planted Carolina Gold—the finest, whitest rice in all the world. And in Charleston, the harbor filled with the masts of two hundred ships, the skyline grew, the steeples of the many churches earning the town the sobriquet "Holy City." Guaranteeing the religious fugitives of Europe the freedom to worship, Charleston soon after it was settled opened its doors to the French Huguenots, Sephardic Jews, and Protestants from the Palatinate who would color the city's English character. Offered land and, upon joining the King's church, a few slaves, Europeans came and made their fortunes in what was all but a rice kingdom.

Everywhere, people planted. The narrow downtown lots

ABOVE AND OPPOSITE: **The ironwork of Charleston is mostly wrought in reserved Federal designs.**

PRECEDING PAGES: **Ionic and Corinthian columns grace a double piazza overlooking the Battery.** LEFT: **The cast-iron bench in the garden of the Nathaniel Russell house is an exception.**

began to fill with the one-room-wide "single house" that would characterize the cityscape. Early Charlestonians embraced the local flora and imported exotica for their gardens. By the middle of the eighteenth century, Charleston gardens were world-renowned, and, fitting with the Georgian era, so was its society. On the eve of the Revolution, the high-walled parterre of a Charleston town house was practically a given. Most houses also had kitchen gardens with a variety of herbs and vegetables matched only by today's garden enthusiasts. Ancient myrtles, camellias, and azaleas are found in Charleston gardens as well as familiar native specimens of magnolia, jasmine, and fern. The art of flower arranging in the city is most often simply a matter of placing garden cuttings in a vase.

Double and triple piazzas, as we call our porches in Charleston, were attached to the single houses in the nineteenth century, adding a tropical element to the architecture while providing an outdoor room that shades the sun and catches the harbor's breezes. The narrow homes, turned sideways to the street, were thus enlarged; a door opens from the sidewalk onto the first floor piazza.

Historic preservation was born in Charleston, whose seal since the seventeenth century has included "She protects her buildings and her customs." In the Historic District, there are hundreds of architecturally significant structures, witnesses to that auspicious creed. Fires, wars, earthquakes, and devastating hurricanes have plagued the city from its inception, but Charleston always, proudly, defends her motto and rebuilds. It's been called the City of Memory, but what Charleston does best, perhaps, is to forget the hard times, when it was "too poor to paint, too proud to whitewash." With its jubilantly restored gardens and homes, it's again the charming little subtropical London that Good King Charles imagined.

OVERLEAF: **An old Charleston graveyard planted with crepe myrtles and live oaks,** LEFT, **and a brick alleyway in the oldest part of town.**

Three O'Clock Dinner at the John Blake House

ABOVE: **The front gate, crowned with trumpet vine.** OPPOSITE: **The dining room set for dinner.**

✛

Cold Curried Squash Soup

Fried Catfish

Butter Beans and Okra

Red Rice

Mixed Green Salad

Plum Tart

✛

WHEN JOHN BLAKE began building his L-shaped house in the late eighteenth century, it sat on the southernmost point of the peninsula that is downtown Charleston. As a successful shipping broker and president of the Bank of South Carolina, Blake entertained in the more formal, second-floor drawing room, where it was cooler and from where he and his guests could look out over the marsh or down into his fashionable, high-walled parterre. The frame house is an unusual variation of the traditional Charleston single house, and, per Georgian custom, is built on a high raised stucco basement. The double piazzas were added in the nineteenth century, long after Blake's death.

Both house and garden have been fully restored to their former

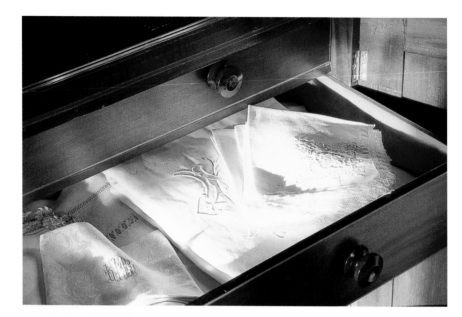

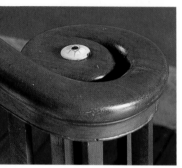

grandeur, with special atten-
tion paid to the furnishings.
Eighteenth-century French
chandeliers, a carving by
Grinling Gibbons, and fine
porcelains complement the
Federal moldings and mantels. The triple-pedestal
mahogany dining table glows in the Georgian yellow
room and is flanked by a rare 1790 Charleston
sideboard.

Three o'clock was traditional dinnertime in
Charleston until very recently. This late summer
meal of fresh local fish, vegetables, and red rice is a
lowcountry classic. A salad of just-picked greens was
dressed simply, with lemon juice and olive oil. Diners
retire to the more formal drawing room, now downstairs, for coffee after an elegant plum tart. Serve a
Vouvray or dry Chenin Blanc with this.

Cold Curried Squash Soup

Try this soup in the late summer, when the winter squash
begin to appear. To make yogurt "cheese" simply drain
plain yogurt in a cheesecloth-lined sieve until it is very
thick. For distinctive, bright curries, it's best to make your
own spice blends, but you can substitute 1 tablespoon of
commercial curry powder if you prefer.

For the curry powder
1 tablespoon coriander seeds
2 teaspoons cumin seeds
2 teaspoons hot red pepper flakes
2 teaspoons ground turmeric
½ teaspoon (about 12) whole cloves
1 small cinnamon stick (about 3 inches)
1 teaspoon black peppercorns
½ teaspoon ground ginger
2 bay leaves

For the soup
1 large acorn or butternut squash (about 2 pounds)
3 tablespoons unsalted butter or olive oil
1 medium onion, chopped
1 carrot, peeled and chopped
1 celery rib, chopped
2 garlic cloves, minced
4 cups chicken or vegetable broth, preferably homemade
Yogurt cheese and chives for garnish

To make the curry, roast the coriander and cumin seeds in
a skillet over medium-high heat until they begin to jump

OPPOSITE: **The Edwardian breakfront doubles as a linen press,** TOP LEFT. **French girandole and gilded Victorian mirror,** TOP RIGHT. **Legend says the ivory button in the banister,** BOTTOM, **means that the house was paid for when it was built.** LEFT: **Squash soup served in gilt English porcelain.** ABOVE: **Old Paris porcelain on a rare 1790 Charleston sideboard.**

around and little whiffs of smoke appear. Do not let them burn. Transfer them immediately to a spice mill or blender, add the remaining ingredients, and grind well. This makes about ¼ cup; store what you don't use in this recipe in an airtight container in a cool, dry cabinet.

To make the soup, preheat the oven to 350°. Cut the squash in half lengthwise and scoop out and discard the seeds. Place cut side down in a glass baking dish. Add water to about ½ inch.

Place the squash in the oven and bake until it is softened, about 45 minutes. Remove the squash from the oven and set aside.

Place the butter in a large heavy sauté pan over

medium-high heat and add the onion, carrot, and celery. Sauté until the vegetables have softened, 10 to 15 minutes, stirring occasionally. In the meantime, scoop the flesh out of the squash.

Add the squash, 1 tablespoon curry powder, the garlic, and the broth to the pan and stir well to combine. Allow to cook over medium heat until the flavors have mingled, about 10 minutes, then transfer the soup to a blender or food processor to puree. Puree well, then chill the soup before serving.

Garnish each dish with a dollop of yogurt cheese and chives.
SERVES 8

Fried Catfish

Nothing is more summery and delicious than perfectly fried fish. When properly prepared, it is equally at home in an elegant setting such as this one or in the more country setting from which the dish evolved. One of the great charms of the lowcountry is this intermingling of both high and low styles.

Here, fried fillets of catfish are crisp and dry on the outside and moist and tender on the inside. You can use any small cleaned fish or fillets for this dish. Lightly coated with seasoned corn flour, the fish are fried to a golden brown in carefully monitored, clean oil. Corn flour (see Sources) is the finest grind of cornmeal; some Louisiana mills market it as "fish fry." If you can't find it, you can make your own by grinding cornmeal more finely in a blender or food processor.

Peanut oil for frying

1½ cups corn flour, preferably stone-ground (see above)

1 teaspoon salt

½ teaspoon freshly ground black pepper

¼ teaspoon cayenne, or to taste

8 catfish or other white-fleshed fish fillets (about 3 pounds)

Pour the oil into a stockpot or Dutch oven to a depth of at least 1½ inches and heat over medium-high heat to 375°. Preheat the oven to 200°. Place wire racks on 2 baking sheets and set aside.

In a wide bowl, mix the corn flour, salt, pepper, and cayenne. Dip each fillet in the seasoned corn flour, coating it all over but shaking off any excess. Carefully lower each piece into the hot oil. Fill the pot, but do not crowd it. The oil should bubble up around each piece of fish. Monitor the temperature closely so that it stays between 365° and 375°. Fry the fillets until they are golden, about 2 or 3 minutes on each side, depending on the thickness.

Remove the fillets from the oil in the same order that they were immersed, using a wire mesh strainer or any tool that will allow you to hold the fish over the pot as excess grease drains back into the pot. When the fish stops dripping, immediately place the pieces on the prepared baking sheets, then place in the oven.

Always wait for the oil to reach the proper temperature again before adding more food to the pot. Continue frying until all of the fish is fried. Serve immediately.

SERVES 8

OPPOSITE: **Catfish, red rice, butter beans, and okra served on Royal Crown Derby.** ABOVE LEFT: **A carving by Grinling Gibbons in the downstairs drawing room.** ABOVE RIGHT: **A nineteenth-century jockey scale.** LEFT: **Coffee in the formal drawing room.**

Butter Beans and Okra

Butter beans are often served over white rice in the lowcountry, but when red rice is on the menu, they stand on their own with a garnish of fresh okra. Charlestonians are passionate about the dozens of varieties of butter beans that are available from the neighboring barrier island farms. Some varieties, such as Sieva (pronounced SIVvy) beans, were growing here when European settlers first arrived; they are the smallest "baby" butter bean.

The beans are cooked in the traditional manner, with a piece of cured pork. A smoked ham hock adds a world of flavor and virtually no fat to the beans, but if you prefer not to add any meat, cook the beans in vegetable or chicken stock.

The okra should be absolutely fresh, bright green, and free of blemishes; if you can't find perfectly tender, small pods, use frozen. Added to the top of the beans in the final stages of cooking, the okra steams in a matter of minutes.

1 smoked ham hock (about 1 pound)
8 cups water
2 pounds shelled butter beans
1 pound fresh, small okra, or 1 10-ounce package of frozen

Place the ham hock and water in a saucepan and bring to a boil. Cook, uncovered, at a low boil until the water is lightly flavored by the meat, about 30 minutes. Add the beans, return to a boil, reduce the heat, and simmer, uncovered, until they are tender, about 25 or 30 minutes.

While the beans are cooking, trim fresh okra stems down to, but not into, the pod. Place frozen okra on a towel to thaw. About five minutes before serving, place the okra lightly on top of the simmering beans and allow to cook through until they are just tender. Serve the beans hot, with a few okra pods on top of each serving of beans.
SERVES 8

Red Rice

It has been said that to know Charleston is to know rice, and this simple tomato pilau (pronounced PERloe, PiLOE, and PERloo) is one of the classic dishes of the old city of rice planters. Self-respecting Charleston cooks make this with beautiful, local vine-ripened tomatoes, available throughout the summer and fall. In winter months, you may be better off using canned. An adulterated version including tomato paste appeared in the Junior League's *Charleston Receipts* of 1950. This older, simpler version is truer to the original "receipt," as recipes are still called in Charleston, with olive oil replacing the traditional bacon.

3 tablespoons olive oil
2 cups long-grain white rice
2 cups vine-ripened tomatoes, peeled and chopped, or
   1 can crushed tomatoes (14½ ounces)
1½ teaspoons salt
1 quart chicken stock, preferably homemade
2 to 3 tablespoons fresh chopped parsley

Place the oil in a stockpot over medium-high heat, add the rice and sauté, stirring constantly. It will begin to turn white after a few minutes; do not let it scorch or brown. Add the tomatoes and continue to sauté until most of the liquid has evaporated. Add the salt and the stock and simmer slowly, covered, for 30 minutes or until the rice is tender. Remove from the heat and allow to sit for a few minutes. Just before serving, fluff the rice with a large fork as you fold in the chopped parsley. Serve immediately.
SERVES 8

OPPOSITE: **Vegetables and rice ready to be served in the kitchen.** LEFT: **Plum tart on the secondary sideboard, an eighteenth-century English piece.**

Place 1¼ cups of the flour, ¼ cup of the sugar, the butter, the egg yolk, and the milk in the work bowl of a food processor and process until the dough forms a ball. If the dough is too wet and sticks to the bowl, add more flour.

Wrap the ball of dough well in plastic wrap and refrigerate for 2 hours. Unwrap the dough, roll it out on a lightly floured surface to a circle about 12 inches in diameter, then gently place the dough into a 10-inch tart pan with a low edge, gently pushing the dough up and slightly over the edges of the pan. Use a rolling pin or the heel of your hand to push the dough out and down onto the edge of the pan to trim any excess dough, then gently squeeze the dough into the edges again between fingertips and thumbs to raise it slightly over the rim. Refrigerate again while you prepare the plums.

Preheat the oven to 350°. Pit the plums and cut them into quarters. Place the plum quarters on the tart shell, beginning on the outer rim and placing them skin side out around the outer edge. Continue filling the shell, working in concentric circles. When the tart is filled, sprinkle it with 2 tablespoons of sugar and bake until golden brown, about 50 or 60 minutes.

Melt the preserves with the brandy or bourbon, then brush the baked tart with the mixture. Allow to cool to room temperature before serving.

SERVES 8

Plum Tart

This simple tart of fresh plums is a light finish to this classic Charleston midday dinner. You can make this dish early in the day and allow it to sit at room temperature.

1½ cups all-purpose flour

¼ cup plus 2 tablespoons sugar

¼ pound (1 stick) chilled unsalted butter, cut into pieces

1 egg yolk

3 tablespoons milk

1 pound fresh plums

⅓ cup plum preserves

2 tablespoons brandy or bourbon

Hunt Breakfast at Halidon Hill

ABOVE: **On the veranda overlooking the river.** OPPOSITE: **A wooden mortar and pestle and the pear chutney in a kitchen window.**

✛

**Ham Biscuits with
Pear Chutney**

Scrambled Eggs

**Pan-Fried Quail with Grits,
Country Ham, and Cream Gravy**

Ambrosia

Creole Café au Lait

✛

ROGER PINCKNEY BUILT the Quinby house in the late eighteenth century and finely outfitted it with the Federal decorations of the time—marbelized baseboards, dentil cornices, a curving mahogany banister, and Adamesque mantels among them. In 1954, Mary Huguenin moved the house four miles downriver through the forest to its current location on Halidon Hill, originally part of neighboring Middleburg Plantation, site of South Carolina's oldest home.

Huguenin was one of the compilers of *Charleston Receipts*, the best-selling cookbook of the Junior League of Charleston, first published in 1950 and in print ever since. She had the kitchen table made from the building's original floor joists; the room itself is practically all heart pine.

ABOVE: **The "big house" in late afternoon.**
OPPOSITE: **Fried quail is served with grits, country ham, and scrambled eggs in the kitchen.** RIGHT: **The mud room in the hunting lodge.**

Outbuildings include barns and a hunting lodge with sixteen beds.

Quail season lasts from Thanksgiving through February. This hearty breakfast, served in the kitchen, is meant for hunters coming in from a chilly hunt.

Pear chutney (see Condiments) is passed with the ham biscuits as eggs are slowly scrambled. The creole café au lait is made from strong coffee and twice-boiled milk.

Ham Biscuits

Country ham (see Sources) is a rare treat for many, but not in the lowcountry, where in addition to being the centerpiece of the Christmas table, it is pan-fried, added to pilaus, ground into pastes, and stuffed into little yeast rolls like these. Also known as bride's biscuits or angel biscuits, these rolls contain both baking powder and yeast, making them a cross between a biscuit and a roll. In this recipe, we stuff half of the biscuits with ham and leave the others plain. Serve warm with pear chutney (see Condiments).

½ pound (about 2 cups) all-purpose flour, preferably a soft southern one such as White Lily (see Sources), plus flour for dusting
½ teaspoon salt
1 teaspoon baking powder
¼ cup chilled lard
1 teaspoon active dry yeast
1¼ cups buttermilk at room temperature
10 to 12 2-inch pieces of country ham slices

Sift the flour, salt, and baking powder into a warmed mixing bowl. Cut the lard into the mixture with a pastry blender or 2 knives until it is evenly distributed. In a separate bowl, stir the yeast into the buttermilk until thoroughly dissolved, then pour the liquid into the flour mixture, stirring well until blended.

Dust a work surface with flour and turn the dough out onto it. Work the dough lightly with floured fingertips until it is smooth and evenly textured. Roll out to about ½ inch thick, then cut into small 1- to 2-inch biscuits with a clean, floured metal biscuit cutter.

Place the biscuits on an ungreased baking pan, cover with a kitchen towel, and allow to rise by about a fourth, about 20 minutes. Preheat the oven to 400°, then bake the biscuits for about 10 minutes. Remove the biscuits from the oven and pry half of them in half with a fork. Stuff a piece of ham into the split biscuits, then return the biscuits to the oven to finish cooking, about 5 minutes more, or until the tops are lightly browned.

MAKES ABOUT 20 BISCUITS

Pan-Fried Quail with Grits, Country Ham, and Cream Gravy

Breakfast isn't breakfast without a pot of grits, and in the lowcountry that means real "country" grits—whole grain and coarsely stone-ground. They take a little longer to cook than those bland, degerminated ones from the grocery store, but they are so creamy and infinitely more flavorful.

Country ham is fried in a dry pan; oil is added to the pan to fry the quail, and gravy is made with the delicious dregs. You can use water, stock, or milk to make the gravy, but in this no-holds-barred version I use cream.

For the grits

2 quarts water

2 tablespoons unsalted butter

1 1/2 teaspoons salt

2 cups stone-ground whole-grain grits (see Sources)

For the country ham, quail, and gravy

2 center slices country ham, cut into 6 pieces

Peanut oil for frying

6 quail (see Sources), dressed and split up the backbone

1/2 cup all-purpose flour

1/2 teaspoon salt

1/2 teaspoon freshly ground black pepper

2 cups cream

ABOVE: **The gun rack in the kitchen.** RIGHT: **Creamy grits and ham biscuits.** OPPOSITE: **Looking out from the formal drawing room,** BOTTOM, **ambrosia,** TOP.

To make the grits, bring the water, butter, and salt to a boil in a stockpot. Slowly add the grits to the pot, stirring. Return to a boil, then reduce to a simmer. Cook the grits, stirring occasionally so that they do not stick or form a skin, until creamy and done to your liking, at least 20 minutes. Many people cook them much, much longer; if you do, you'll probably have to add more water.

When the grits are almost done, turn the heat to its lowest setting and cover the pot while you prepare the country ham, quail, and gravy.

Preheat the oven to 200°. In a large cast-iron skillet over medium-high heat, fry the country ham slices until they are browned and warmed through. Do not overcook them. Remove them to a platter and place in the warm oven.

Pour peanut oil in the skillet to a depth of about ¾ inch and continue to heat over medium-high. While the oil is heating, pat the quail dry. Place the flour, salt, and pepper in a paper bag and shake well to mix, then add 1 or 2 quail to the bag at a time, shaking well to coat the birds in flour. Shake any excess flour off the birds and place as many of the birds in the hot oil as will fit. Fry until golden brown, about 5 minutes on each side, turning once. Remove the birds to the platter in the oven and continue frying until all of the birds are cooked.

When the last bird has been cooked, pour the oil out of the pan through a sieve and into a heatproof container. Discard after it has cooled. Return the little golden dregs to the frying pan, add the cream, and reduce over high heat, stirring, until the gravy is thickened.

Remove the platter from the oven, place a serving of grits on each plate, then add a quail and a piece of ham to each plate. Pour gravy over the grits and quail and serve immediately.

SERVES 6

Ambrosia

Quail-hunting season coincides with the height of the citrus season. This favored holiday fruit salad complements the hearty breakfast fare. The recipe makes twice as much as you'll need for this meal, but it will keep for a day or two in the refrigerator. If you can't use freshly grated coconut, buy frozen unsweetened flaked coconut.

1 large white grapefruit
1 large red grapefruit
6 large seedless oranges
1 pineapple
1 small coconut, or 6 ounces frozen flaked coconut (about 1¼ cups), thawed

Peel the citrus, then cut each section free of all membranes, allowing the sections to fall into the bowl. Squeeze excess juice from the core and membranes into another container, then drink it while it is fresh. Peel and core the pineapple and cut it into small chunks, adding them to the citrus. Crack the coconut and grate the interior white flesh (most easily done with a rotary grater available at Indian grocers) and add it to the fruit. Toss to mix well. Serve chilled or at room temperature.

SERVES 12

Creole Café au Lait

Take a head count of drinkers and prepare a pot of coffee your usual way, making it a bit stronger; then offer this authentic creole café au lait in mugs.

Strong, freshly brewed coffee
½ cup milk per person

While the coffee is brewing, bring the milk to a boil in a large, heavy saucepan. Watch it carefully and remove it from the heat the moment it comes to a full boil so that it doesn't boil over. When the bubbles have subsided, return the milk to the heat and allow it to come to a full boil again, removing it from the heat again so that it doesn't boil over.

Strain the milk into the mugs with equal parts of coffee. Serve immediately.

OPPOSITE: **The curving mahogany banister.** ABOVE: **A settee in the hallway.** LEFT: **An old engraving of the house.**

Soup in the Kitchen of the Benjamin Phillips House

✝

Pickled Shrimp

Okra Soup with Steamed Rice

Green Bean and Benne Salad

Cornbread

Lemon Squares

✝

CHARLESTON WAS NEVER just planters; the oldest parts of the city are filled with the lovely homes of merchants, such as this one built by Benjamin Phillips in 1818. A variation of the single house, it is entered by a hall that runs down the south side of the house. There is a graceful Georgian arch at the end of the hallway leading into the dining room, where naively hand-painted wallpaper depicts a river, appropriate to the Charleston peninsula.

The home has been meticulously restored and decorated in Colonial Revival fashion. Early American school portraits adorn the walls, and an impressive collection of eighteenth-century porcelains and fine period antiques are displayed throughout the house.

OPPOSITE: **The primitive kitchen table set for lunch.** ABOVE: **Okra soup, green bean salad, and cornbread.**

In contrast, this simple meal of the old Charleston favorite, okra soup and cornbread, is served in the kitchen, once a separate building now cleverly attached to the main house. Above the primitive table, the portrait is a benevolent spirit in the room that looks into the garden filled with confederate jasmine. Lemon squares are served on the one small piazza upstairs,

overlooking the stunning formal garden.

Serve this meal any time of the year, with a crisply dry rosé wine such as those from Provence. Pickled shrimp (see Condiments) are served as an appetizer.

LEFT: **Chinese armorial porcelain from the late eighteenth century in a dining room niche.** BELOW: **Colonial Revival settee and Chinese export porcelain in the second story formal drawing room.**

Okra Soup with Steamed Rice

This delicious soup, bolstered by a rich beef broth made from meaty shin bones, is a lowcountry classic. The recipe makes more than four servings but is delicious reheated for days to come. Begin the broth at least one day before serving, then finish the soup on the second day. Okra soup is always served over steaming white rice (see page 44), cooked lowcountry style so that each grain is separate. If you can't find perfectly vine-ripened tomatoes and blemish-free okra, buy canned tomatoes and cut-up frozen okra. They'll be better than inferior "fresh" products.

1 large, meaty beef shank bone, cut into 3-inch pieces,
    with a marrow bone (3 to 5 pounds)
5 quarts water
1 large onion, chopped
5 cups vine-ripened tomatoes (about 3 pounds),
    peeled and chopped, or 1 28-ounce can tomatoes plus
    1 14½-ounce can high-quality tomatoes
1 bay leaf
1 fresh thyme sprig, or ½ teaspoon dried
3 pounds fresh or frozen okra, cut into pieces
Fresh lemon juice and salt to taste
Bottled hot sauce to taste

Place the shank pieces in a large stockpot and cover with water. Bring to a boil, immediately reduce the heat, and simmer, uncovered, for about 2 hours, skimming the surface of scum frequently. When the meat is tender and falling from the bones, remove the stock from the heat and allow to cool. Remove the bones and refrigerate the broth. Pick the meat from the bones, cover the meat, and refrigerate. Discard the bones.

The next day, remove the congealed fat from the surface of the broth, discarding all but about 2 or 3 tablespoons. Place enough of the fat in the bottom of a Dutch oven to cover the surface and melt over medium heat. Add the onion and sauté until transparent, about 10 minutes. Add the tomatoes and the herbs and continue to cook, stirring frequently, until most of the liquid has cooked out, about 20 minutes. Add the okra, the reserved meat, and 3 quarts of the reserved broth, and cook for another 20 minutes, until the soup is warmed through and the okra is just beginning to break down. Adjust the seasoning with lemon juice, salt, and hot sauce, then serve over steamed rice, passing the hot sauce.

SERVES 8 TO 12

Green Bean and Benne Salad

Another Charleston favorite, this salad of green beans tossed with sesame seeds—"benne" to Charlestonians—is best when served at room temperature. Benne came with the slave trade from West Africa early on and has been firmly entrenched in lowcountry cooking for three hundred years. The salad is brightened with hot peppers, which though native to the New World had long been in favor in the West African countries whence came the slaves.

1½ pounds fresh young green beans, stemmed but
    with the tender tip intact
3 tablespoons sesame seeds
½ teaspoon crushed red pepper, or to taste
3 tablespoons extra-virgin olive oil
1 or 2 garlic cloves, minced, to taste
Salt and freshly ground black pepper to taste
4 teaspoons fresh lemon juice

Plunge the green beans into a pot of rapidly boiling water and cook them, uncovered, until they become just tender and lose their raw flavor, about 4 minutes. Immediately dump them into a colander in the sink and run cold water over them to stop the cooking and so that they retain their bright green color. Set aside to drain.

Place the sesame seeds in a dry heavy skillet over medium heat. Pan-roast them, stirring occasionally, until they are evenly brown all over. Remove them from the pan and mix with the remaining ingredients except the lemon juice. If serving the salad immediately, add the lemon juice as well and toss the beans with the dressing. If serving the salad later, dress the salad without the lemon juice (which can discolor the beans) and refrigerate until about 30 minutes before serving. Add the lemon juice at the last minute, tossing well.

SERVES 6

BELOW: **Steaming white rice.**
RIGHT: **A perfect slice of cornbread.**
OPPOSITE: **Hepplewhite settee and
a late eighteenth-century American
School portrait; a globe lantern
hangs from the original plaster ceiling
medallion.**

Cornbread

This is the best cornbread you'll ever
eat—truly southern, with no wheat
flour or sugar, baked in a sizzling hot
cast-iron skillet seasoned with a little
bacon fat for that golden brown crust.
It will be infinitely better if you use whole-grain, stone-
ground cornmeal (see Sources).

You will need a 9- or 10-inch, well-seasoned, never-
washed cast iron skillet for this recipe.

1½ to 2 teaspoons strained bacon grease
1 egg
2 cups buttermilk at room temperature
1¾ cups cornmeal, preferably whole-grain, stone-ground
1 scant teaspoon salt
1 scant teaspoon baking powder
1 scant teaspoon baking soda

Add enough bacon grease to the skillet to coat the bottom
of the pan, then put it in a cold oven and preheat to 450°.
In the meantime, mix the egg into the buttermilk, then add
the cornmeal and mix well.

After about 10 minutes, when the oven has reached
450°, the grease should be just to the smoking point.
Quickly stir the salt, baking powder, and soda into the
batter and add the batter all at once to the hot pan. Bake
for 15 to 20 minutes, or until the top just begins to brown.
Turn the bread out onto a platter and serve hot with lots
of butter.

MAKES 8 TO 10 SLICES TO SERVE 6

Lemon Squares

These are very old-fashioned lemon squares, made with real lemon curd and shortbread. Citrus trees were popular in eighteenth-century Charleston gardens; on some of the plantations, the owners built orangeries to protect the trees from occasional winter freezes. The Meyer lemon, a large sweet variety, is a favored variety today for courtyard gardens. Though shunned by commercial growers because it carries a disease that damages other citrus, Meyer lemons are large, sweet, and juicy. Use them for this dessert if you can find them.

The semolina or rice flour is added for texture, per old Scottish recipes. If you use rice flour, it should be a fairly coarse, natural product, not the processed Southeast Asian type.

2 or 3 lemons, or 1 large Meyer lemon

5 egg yolks

1 cup sugar, well sifted

½ pound (2 sticks) unsalted butter at room temperature

¼ teaspoon salt

1 cup all-purpose flour, well sifted

¼ cup semolina or rice flour

Confectioners' sugar (optional)

Grate the zest from 2 lemons onto a sheet of wax paper and set aside. Squeeze ⅓ cup of lemon juice into a measuring cup. If you don't have ⅓ cup, squeeze juice from another lemon. In the top of a double boiler or in a wide stainless-steel bowl that will fit over a saucepan, beat the egg yolks with the lemon juice and zest and ¾ cup of the sugar. Save the wax paper.

Put the bowl over simmering water and whisk the mixture until it is very thick and light in color, about 7 minutes. Remove from the heat and gradually beat in one of the sticks of butter, a little at a time. The mixture should be very shiny and smooth. Set aside while you make the shortbread.

Preheat the oven to 325°. Cream the remaining stick of butter and ¼ cup sugar together with the salt in a mixing bowl. Add the flour and the semolina or rice flour and mix well. Turn the mixture out into an 8-inch square baking pan and cover with the wax paper. Press evenly into the pan, then remove the wax paper.

Bake for 20 minutes, then remove from the oven. Add the lemon curd and bake another 10 minutes. Remove from the oven and place on a rack to cool completely before cutting into sixteen 2-inch squares. Dust with confectioners' sugar if desired.

MAKES 16 SQUARES

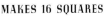

OPPOSITE: **Confederate jasmine entwines the column and garden gate.** LEFT: **Lemon squares are served in an informal upstairs drawing room overlooking the garden.** ABOVE: **The lemon squares.**

RICE

IF YOU TRAVEL in an airplane between Charleston and Savannah, you can see traces of the old rice plantations in the watery grids that line the lowcountry's rivers. It's a testament to the enormous engineering skills of West African slaves, who were the real masters of rice growing. All along the rivers a series of banks and canals that impound the rice fields were carved out of the subtropical jungle. The anthropologist Leland Ferguson has shown that the movement of earth that was necessary for the rice plantations in the lowcountry was greater in volume than the Egyptian pyramid at Cheops, the world's largest. By the outbreak of the Civil War, nearly all of the nation's five million bushels of rice exported annually were being grown in the lowcountry.

Planters built not only their "big houses" on the plantations but fancy town houses where they entertained lavishly. The rice brokers, merchants, and lawyers became wealthy, too, in the upwardly spiraling economy that was founded on the humble grain. Early on, the colony had not only a black majority, but the largest black majority of all the colonies. The wealthy lowcountry elite owed everything to the West African field hands, cooks, and carpenters, who taught them the marsh cultivation and preparation of rice that was practiced in their homelands. Today, though it hasn't been grown commercially in the lowcountry in several generations, rice is still the starch of choice here. Though there is a rice steamer that many locals use, the traditional West African method of cooking perfect rice—lowcountry style, so that each grain is separate—is still the easiest and most common technique:

Use one part long-grain white rice to two parts cold water. Add a little salt and allow the pot to simmer, covered, for exactly thirteen minutes without lifting the lid. Turn off the heat and allow the pot to stand for another twelve minutes. Lift the lid and fluff the rice with a fork, separating the grains. Never stir the rice with a spoon!

OPPOSITE:
Ruins of the oldest rice mill in the lowcountry, at Middleburg Plantation.

Sunday Dinner at the Vincent Le Seigneur House

✛

She-Crab Soup
Roast Squab
Steamed Broccoli
Fried Eggplant
Sweet Potato Cake

✛

ABOVE: **The sideboard is set for coffee with blue and white porcelain cups and a Sheraton urn.** OPPOSITE: **Flowers from the garden brighten each place setting.**

DR. VINCENT LE SEIGNEUR built his fine single house in 1819, embellishing it in the late Adam style. The house is situated in one of the city's oldest neighborhoods, surrounded by a high stuccoed wall.

Outbuildings include a kitchen and slave quarters, now attached to the house, and a pigeonnier now used as a pool house.

The Le Seigneur house has handsome wood- and plasterwork, fanlights, ceiling medallions, and architraves. Fluted columns support a double piazza that overlooks a delightful garden that provides cut flowers for spring dinners such as this one. The broccoli is steamed until just tender, then lightly dressed with high-quality extra-virgin olive oil just as it is sent to the table. Sherry is offered both before the meal and with the soup. With the meal, pour a Provence rouge or a Burgundy at least six years old.

She-Crab Soup

No dish is more profoundly lowcountry. Many versions thicken the soup with flour, but this old version is based on its Scottish antecedent, *partan bree*, and is thickened with rice. If you can't get fresh crabs, make a rich shellfish stock with shrimp and lobster shells (you can freeze them until you have enough), then add fresh crabmeat and roe (see Sources) as you send the soup bowls to the table.

Don't worry if your crabs don't yield a full pound of meat or quarter pound of roe. The soup will be delicious nonetheless.

3 quarts water
1½ tablespoons crab or shrimp boil, such as Old Bay Seasoning
Salt
12 to 14 large female blue crabs
2⅓ cups long-grain white rice
1 quart milk
1 cup cream
Cayenne pepper and freshly ground black pepper to taste
Amontillado sherry

Bring the water to a rolling boil and add the seafood boil, 2 teaspoons salt, and the crabs. Boil for 30 minutes, then remove the crabs, reserving 1 cup of the cooking water. Pick the crabs, which should yield about 1 pound of meat and ¼ pound of roe. The roe is bright orange and is packed throughout the shell.

Cook the rice in the milk at a low boil until the rice is very soft, about 30 minutes. Strain the mixture or puree very fine, then return it to the pot. Add the reserved crab water and the cream and heat the mixture through. Season to taste with a dash of cayenne, salt, and pepper. Fill bowls with the soup, add a dollop of crabmeat and a generous sprinkling of roe to each, and finish each bowl with a spoonful of sherry.
SERVES 6

ABOVE LEFT: **She-crab soup and sherry.**
LEFT: **Roast squab, steamed broccoli, and fried eggplant.**

Roast Squab

The pigeonnier behind the Le Seigneur house once provided plenty of squab for the table. Young pigeons that have not yet grown feathers, the succulent squab have been raised on pure springwater and whole grains at Palmetto Pigeon in Sumter, South Carolina, since 1923.

The birds often appear in lowcountry pilaus, but this simple roasting best shows off their unique flavor. Nothing could be easier to prepare.

6 squabs, about ³/₄ pound each (see Sources, page 173)
¹/₄ cup extra-virgin olive oil
Salt and freshly ground black pepper to taste

Preheat the oven to 425°. Trim the wing tips. Rinse the birds well; pat dry, then rub each bird well both inside and out with the oil. Salt and pepper the birds inside and out, then tie the legs together with kitchen twine. Place the birds in a roasting pan and place in the oven.

Roast the birds until the skin is golden brown and the juices run clear from the leg joint when it is pierced with a knifepoint, about 20 minutes. Remove from the oven, place a piece of aluminum foil loosely over the birds, and allow to rest for 5 minutes. Just before serving, slit the string that binds the legs with a knife and remove.

SERVES 6

ABOVE: **The lower piazza.**

Fried Eggplant

This version of fried eggplant—famous in southern countries around the world—is really eggplant home fries. Placing the eggplant in a saltwater bath for a little while will remove any bitterness the larger vegetables sometimes have. Be sure to buy firm ones with bright green tops; they're less likely to have seeds.

2 large, very firm eggplants
Salt
Peanut oil for frying
¹/₂ cup fine white cornmeal or corn flour

About 45 minutes before serving, peel the eggplants and cut them as for home fries (large irregular fries). Place them in a bowl of salted ice water for about 30 minutes.

Preheat the oven to 200°. Place a wire rack over a baking sheet and place it in the oven. Drain the eggplant well. Pour at least 2 inches of oil into a stockpot or Dutch oven and place over medium-high heat. Put the cornmeal or corn flour in a shallow bowl and dredge the eggplant well, dusting off any excess. When the oil has reached 365°, fry the eggplant in batches until golden brown, about 3 minutes. Remove to the prepared baking sheet in the oven to drain and to stay warm while you finish the frying. Serve immediately.

SERVES 6

ABOVE: **Looking out from the upstairs drawing room into the piazza and street beyond.** RIGHT: **A detail of the architrave in the formal drawing room.**

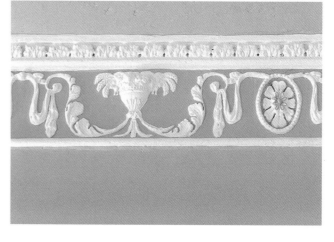

ABOVE: **Sweet potato cake, served from the sideboard.**

Sweet Potato Cake

This wonderful cake is made with olive oil instead of butter. It is light and moist and keeps well. Make sure all of your ingredients are at room temperature before you begin. If your mixer has only one bowl, beat the egg whites first, then turn them out into another bowl—preferably copper— while you continue with the dish. Use a 10-inch tube pan for this cake, but don't grease it: you want the batter to cling to the sides and rise high. Nonstick pans with removable inserts work particularly well with this recipe.

1 cup fruity olive oil

2 cups sugar

4 eggs, separated

½ cup hot water

2¼ cups soft southern flour (see Sources) or cake flour

1 large sweet potato, peeled and grated (2½ to 3 cups)

1 teaspoon baking powder

1 teaspoon baking soda

½ teaspoon salt

1 teaspoon ground ginger

1 teaspoon ground freshly grated nutmeg

1 teaspoon vanilla extract

Preheat the oven to 350°.

In the large bowl of an electric mixer, beat the oil with the sugar until it is well mixed. Use the paddle attachment if your mixer has one. Add the egg yolks, one at a time, beating well after each. Slowly pour in the hot water and continue to beat until the mixture is light.

Sift ¼ cup of the flour over the sweet potato in a large bowl and toss so that it is lightly coated. This will keep the potato from sinking to the bottom of the cake.

Sift the remaining flour with the baking powder, soda, salt, ginger, and nutmeg. Add the dry to the wet ingredients and mix well, then mix in the vanilla and the sweet potatoes.

Beat the egg whites until they hold stiff peaks, then fold them gently but thoroughly into the batter. Pour the batter into a 10-inch tube pan and bake for 1 hour, or until the cake is lightly browned and a straw poked into the cake comes out clean. Remove from the oven, invert the pan, and allow to cool completely.

SERVES 12

Spring Dinner at the William Gibbes House

ABOVE: **Looking out the basement door toward the gardens.**
OPPOSITE: **Shrimp creole and sweet potato corn muffins.**

✝

Blackeyed Pea Cakes with
Roasted Red Pepper Puree

Sweet Potato Corn Muffins

Shrimp Creole

Pears Poached in Champagne

✝

WHEN THE WEALTHY MERCHANT planter Gibbes began building his Georgian mansion on the Ashley River in 1772, it overlooked his huge, thriving wharf to the south and his fancy parterred gardens to the rear. Late in the eighteenth century he sold the house to Sarah Moore Smith, who added putty ornaments to mantels and door surrounds and an unusual wrought iron balustrade to the staircase. Mrs. Smith also added the majestic double marble exterior staircase that now looks not over the river, but onto a lovely city street, the marshes having been filled in over the past two hundred years to make way for downtown property.

In the 1920s, Cornelia Roebling, widow of the builder of the Brooklyn Bridge, returned to her native South Carolina and saved the Gibbes

house from a deteriorated state. Grand became grander under Mrs. Roebling's direction as she extended the rear of the house, remodeled the southeastern parlor in Chinese Chippendale style, added elegant wallpapers, and hired the great landscape architect Loutrel Briggs to restore the vast gardens to their colonial grandeur. A huge live oak now dominates the principal courtyard to the rear of the house, where the original kitchen and carriage houses stand fully restored, gorgeously patinaed. The gardens provide native and exotic flowers for the table throughout the year. This dinner is served at the height of spring, when wisteria, azaleas, and spirea are in full bloom. Serve with a Barbera d'Alba.

ABOVE LEFT: **The rear landing of the staircase.** LEFT: **Door surrounds in the front drawing rooms.** ABOVE: **Looking into the dining room, which is set for dinner.**

Blackeyed Pea Cakes with Roasted Red Pepper Puree

Recipes for pan-fried bean cakes are legion in the low-country, where over three hundred varieties of beans—many called "peas"—are grown. You can use any leftover beans you like in this dish. Frozen blackeyed peas work just fine. If you use canned beans such as black beans, be sure that they contain nothing but beans, water, and salt, and rinse them well.

The roasted pepper puree contains wine. If you are making the entire menu, you can use some of the champagne called for in the pear recipe. If you can't get fresh herbs, use 1 teaspoon of dried mixed herbs such as herbes de Provence or Italian seasoning. I use fresh parsley, oregano, thyme, basil, and sage and garnish the serving platter with sprigs of the herbs to signify flavors.

For the red pepper puree
4 ripe large red bell peppers
1 shallot, finely chopped
3/4 cup dry white wine
About 1/4 cup fresh parsley leaves
Salt and freshly ground black pepper

For the pea cakes
2 cups cooked and drained blackeyed peas or beans
    of your choice
1 egg, separated
1 tablespoon chopped fresh herbs of your choice
6 small scallions, white and some green, chopped
1 garlic clove, minced
1 hot pepper such as a jalapeño, seeded and minced, or a
    bottled hot pepper sauce, to taste (optional)
1/4 teaspoon cumin or chili powder
Salt and freshly ground black pepper
3/4 cup fine dry bread crumbs
3 tablespoons peanut or olive oil or clarified butter
    for frying

To make the pepper puree, roast the peppers in a very hot oven or on gas burners until the skin blisters and turns black. Burn only the skin, not the flesh, of the peppers. Turn them so that they roast evenly all over. Place the roasted peppers in a sealed bag or in a covered bowl for at least 10 minutes so that the skins steam away from the flesh. Peel away the skins, then pull the stem end away and discard. Scrape away the seeds. Cut up 1/4 cup of the

ABOVE: **Appetizers are served on a bowfront chest in the dining room.**

roasted peppers and set them aside for the pea cakes.

Place the shallot and wine in a saucepan, reduce by half, and remove from the heat. Place the parsley on a cutting board and sprinkle liberally with salt. Chop fine. You should have about 2 tablespoons. Add the chopped parsley and the roasted peppers to the wine reduction and puree until smooth. Season to taste with salt and pepper and serve as soon as possible, thinning with a little wine if necessary.

To make the cakes, mash the beans with a large fork in a bowl, then add the egg yolk and mix well. Add the remaining ingredients except the egg white, bread crumbs, and oil. Fold in 1/2 cup of the bread crumbs.

Beat the egg white to soft peaks and fold it into the mixture.

Heat the oil in a skillet over medium-high heat. Mold 12 small patties in your hands, placing each down in the bread crumbs, coating both sides well. Fry the cakes until golden brown all over, about 2 minutes on each side. Serve immediately with the puree.

SERVES 6

Sweet Potato Corn Muffins

These bright orange breads combine two of the lowcountry's favorite foodstuffs, sweet potatoes and cornmeal.

4 tablespoons (½ stick) unsalted butter, melted
¾ cup mashed baked sweet potato
2 cups buttermilk at room temperature
1 egg
1¾ cups stone-ground whole-grain cornmeal
1 teaspoon baking powder
1 teaspoon baking soda
1 teaspoon salt

Paint the insides of twelve 2½-inch muffin cups (preferably a nonstick tin) with a little of the melted butter, place in a cold oven, and preheat to 425°. While the oven is preheating, mix the sweet potato well into the buttermilk, then add the egg and mix well. Add the cornmeal and mix well again.

When the oven is preheated, quickly mix in the baking powder, soda, and salt, then stir in the melted butter. Pour the batter into the muffin tin, dividing it evenly among the 12 cups. Bake for 15 minutes, or until the tops just begin to brown. Turn the muffins out into a cloth-lined basket and serve at once.
MAKES 12 MUFFINS

Shrimp Creole

This is classic lowcountry creole cooking, Caribbean in origin and now a favorite throughout the South. The secret to any good shrimp dish is to not overcook the shrimp. As with the pea cakes, you can flavor the dish to suit your own palate by your choice of herbs.

2¼ cups long-grain white rice
¼ cup olive oil
1½ cups chopped onion (about 1 large)
¾ cup chopped bell pepper (about 1 medium)
1 large jalapeño pepper, seeded and minced
¾ cup chopped celery (about 2 ribs)
1 tablespoon chopped fresh herbs of your choice, or 1
    teaspoon mixed dried herbs, such as herbes de Provence
    or Italian seasoning, crushed
3 garlic cloves, minced
6 cups peeled and chopped tomatoes (about 6 or 7 large)
Salt and freshly ground black pepper
2½ pounds shrimp, peeled
Fresh lemon juice (optional)

Cook the rice lowcountry style, so that each grain stands separately (see page 44). While the rice is cooking, warm the oil in a large sauté pan over medium-high heat and add the onion, peppers, celery, herbs, and garlic. Cook until the vegetables are soft, stirring occasionally, about 10 minutes.

Add the tomatoes and cook until most of the juice has cooked out and the flavors are well mingled, about 10 minutes more. Adjust the seasoning with salt and pepper.

Just before serving, add the shrimp and stir them well into the sauce. Cook until they are just cooked, no more than 5 minutes (depending on their size). Taste again for seasoning, sprinkling with a little lemon juice if desired. Serve immediately over the hot rice.
SERVES 6

Pears Poached in Champagne

When the mint pokes through the ground in the spring, I love to poach pears and garnish them with sprigs to resemble leaves. There's no simpler, or prettier, dessert. You can serve these warm, chilled, or at room temperature.

1 large lemon
1⅓ cups sugar, plus about 2 teaspoons for garnish
2 cups champagne
6 coriander seeds
4 tablespoons (½ stick) unsalted butter
6 firm pears, peeled
6 sprigs fresh mint, for garnish

Cut several long zests of lemon to use as a garnish, sprinkle with 1 teaspoon sugar, and set aside. Quarter the lemon and add it to the champagne, 1⅓ cups sugar, coriander,

OPPOSITE: **The owner uses flowers from the Briggs-designed gardens throughout the house.** ABOVE: **Pears poached in champagne.**

and butter in a heavy saucepan that has a lid. Add the pears and simmer, covered, until the pears are tender and translucent, 25 to 45 minutes. Turn the pears over carefully when the underside is done. The time will vary according to the variety and ripeness of the pears.

Remove the pears from the pot to a serving dish and set aside. Increase the heat and reduce the poaching liquid until it thickens. Remove from the heat and pour over the pears, straining out the solids. You may refrigerate them at this point if desired.

Just before serving, sprinkle the lemon zests with another teaspoon of sugar, stick a sprig of mint in each pear, and garnish the pears with the lemon zests.
SERVES 6

BEAUFORT

BEAUTIFUL BEAUFORT BY THE SEA it's called, and not without reason. Nestled in among live oaks in a wide oxbow on the inland barrier island of Port Royal at the head of a system of creeks and estuaries called the Beaufort River, the once sleepy southern town is one of the loveliest on the East Coast. Beaufort is surrounded by islands and hammocks—small forested clumps of land amid the vast salt marshes. Just south of it lies Port Royal Sound, named in 1562 by the French explorer Jean Ribault, whose short-lived colony on Parris Island was the second of several attempted settlements of Beaufort prior to the permanent English one of the early eighteenth century. The sound receives the Broad River that separates Hilton Head and St. Helena Islands on the coast, a few miles downstream.

Many flags have flown over Beaufort (pronounced BEWfort). One of the earliest landings by Europeans in the New World was by the Spanish at St. Helena Island; there are tabby ruins. Peculiar to the area, tabby is an ingenious concrete made mostly from oyster shells. It continued to be used in Beaufort long after all other Spanish influences had disappeared: it was used in all of the homes featured in this chapter. The town of Beaufort was founded in 1711 by English planters and traders whose indigo would make them very wealthy. Escaping the malaise of the marshlands in summer, the planters began to build their houses in the town. After the Revolution, rice and Sea Island cotton became the important crops, with Port Royal and St. Helena Islands becoming the seats of huge cotton plantations. The grand homes in Beaufort are a testament to the vast wealth of those planters.

Beaufort had more than four thousand inhabitants before 1800. By then, it was being called "the wealthiest, most aristocratic and cultivated town of its size in America." All but one of

PRECEDING PAGE: **Palmettos rustle in the breeze aside this bay-front portico.** ABOVE: **A corner of an informal garden.** BELOW: **Plants on a portico.** RIGHT: **The Oaks, an Italianate home built in 1856.**

ABOVE: **A Victorian porch with ceiling fan.** BELOW: **This 1860 home has been moved twice from its original location.**

the Beaufort houses included in this collection were built prior to the nineteenth century. The one exception, the Secession House, was built in 1813 on tabby foundations dating to 1724. All have contributed to a loose architectural style known as Beaufort. Unlike the single houses of Charleston that are turned sideways on their skinny lots, or the upright Regency row houses of Savannah, Beaufort developed a few idiosyncratic residential features that set it apart from the beginning. Raised on a high, often arched, stuccoed tabby basement, the Beaufort house sits regally in the center of a large lot, often a city block deep. As the homes became grander in the Georgian tradition, they adopted a T-shape, with rear rooms perpendicular to those at the front of the house, so that all rooms have that breezy southern exposure. Even the earliest homes had deep porches on their south sides, shading the front rooms and catching the sea breezes. In the Federal era, Adamesque details were added.

Even more so than Charleston, Beaufort can be defined by its porches, which have been incorporated by the builders with every passing style. The city today, with its avid gardeners, its breathtaking views, and its lovely homes, is truly a gem among the Sea Islands.

OPPOSITE: **Spanish moss sways in the breeze at the Robert Means house on the bay.**

Frogmore Stew at Tombee Plantation

ABOVE: **Frogmore stew includes fresh shrimp, corn, and local smoked sausage.** OPPOSITE: **Looking out of the house toward the dock.**

✚

Boiled Peanuts

The Best Lemonade

Frogmore Stew

Pita Bread

Cole Slaw

Scuppernong Pie

Red Velvet Cake

✚

THOMAS B. CHAPLIN built his remote country home on a bend in Station Creek on St. Helena Island about 1795, when his long-staple cotton plantation was thriving. The journal that his grandson kept fifty years later is an important document of plantation life and the social customs of the Sea Islands, brilliantly annotated in Ted Rosengarten's prizewinning *Tombee: Portrait of a Cotton Planter.* The younger Chaplin enjoyed food, drink, and the companionship of neighboring planters more than he did farming, bookkeeping, and management; his life was a continual struggle, tempered by booze and billiards.

The T-shaped house is raised on tabby columns above a submerged basement, unusual for the low-country. Its wide double portico catches the southern breezes, and the property, now shaded with giant live oaks and cedars, is virtually surrounded by salt marsh creeks and inlets. The interior features some early Adam gougework and delightfully feathered wain-scoting, but the T shape affords windows in every room, drawing the eye out of the relatively small house.

Nowhere is there a more beautiful setting for this favored lowcountry meal of "Frogmore Stew." Also known as "Beaufort Stew" or "Lowcountry Boil," the dish is closely akin to New England's seafood boils; Frogmore is the old township name on St. Helena.

The meal is a celebration of late summer's bounty. For the "stew," local smoked sausage, shrimp, and just-picked corn are warmed together outdoors in a large pot of seasoned water. Boiled peanuts are served with beer and lemonade beforehand. Quite often the picnic tables are covered with newspapers to catch the shrimp peels and corn cobs. Homemade pita bread and cole slaw accompany the boil. Beer is the drink of choice.

The desserts are both peculiarly southern: scuppernong pie, made with the local slip-skin grapes, and the ubiquitous red velvet cake.

PRECEDING PAGES: **Live oaks and the surrounding marsh,** LEFT. **The porches of Tombee are nearly always breezy,** RIGHT. OPPOSITE: **A stately palmetto, the South Carolina state tree.** ABOVE: **Live oaks and palmettos.**

Boiled Peanuts

This may be the favored lowcountry snack—certainly for casual outdoor affairs such as this one, where the shells can be tossed on the ground. They take several hours to cook and cure, so start them well in advance of your guests' arrival. If you're preparing Frogmore Stew outdoors, you can use the same cooker for the peanuts that you'll use for the shrimp boil.

If you don't live in a peanut-growing region, ask an Indian grocer to get you some. Figure a pound per beer drinker.

8 pounds freshly dug green peanuts in the shell
8 tablespoons salt
2 gallons water

Cook the peanuts, uncovered, over a low boil in the salted water for 1 to 2 hours, until they are cooked to your liking. Add more water if necessary.

Let the peanuts sit in the water until the desired degree of saltiness is reached (10 minutes to 1 hour), then drain them and put them near the drinks. They're good warm or cool, and can be frozen.

The Best Lemonade

If you've had better lemonade, please send me the recipe! Make this at least an hour before your guests arrive, then garnish with fresh mint sprigs.

6 juicy lemons
1 cup sugar
6 cups water
Fresh mint sprigs

Scrub the lemons with a little soapy water to remove any oil or wax coatings. Rinse them well. Cut the lemons in half and put them in a 2-quart heat-resistant pitcher. Add the cup of sugar.

Bring the water to a boil and pour it over the lemons, stirring to dissolve the sugar. As soon as the lemons are cool enough to handle (30 or 40 minutes), squeeze the juice out of them into the pitcher. Discard the lemons. Refrigerate until use.

Pour the lemonade into iced glasses, garnishing with sprigs of mint.
SERVES 8

Frogmore Stew

This is an easy way to feed a crowd, and it's absolutely delicious if you have fresh shrimp and corn and don't over-cook them. If they don't make spicy smoked sausages in your neck of the woods, use any smoked sausage such as Kielbasa and add some crushed red pepper to the recipe.

3 tablespooons shrimp or crab boil, such as Old Bay
   Seasoning
3 tablespoons salt
1 ½ gallons water
2 pounds hot smoked link sausage, cut into 2-inch pieces
12 ears freshly shucked corn, broken into 3- to 4-inch pieces
4 pounds fresh shrimp

In a large stockpot, add the shrimp boil and salt to the water and bring to a boil. Add the sausage and boil, uncovered, for 5 minutes. Add the corn and count 5 minutes. Add the shrimp and count 3 minutes. Do not wait for the liquid to come to a boil when timing the corn and shrimp. Drain immediately and serve.
SERVES 8

ABOVE: **Sunset over the marsh.** OPPOSITE: **Boiled peanuts and Frogmore stew are lowcountry favorites.**

Pita Bread

Pita bread is both easy and fun to make. Start the dough
several hours before your party or make it early in the day.

2 teaspoons active dry yeast
½ teaspoon sugar
2½ cups warm water, about 110° to 120°
2 pounds unbleached all-purpose flour (about 7 cups),
    plus flour for dusting
1 tablespoon salt
Olive oil

Dissolve the yeast and sugar in about ½ cup of water and
leave in a warm place for about 10 minutes to proof. It
should be slightly bubbly and smell freshly of yeast.

In a large warmed mixing bowl, mix the flour and salt.
Make a well in the center, add the yeast mixture, and stir
thoroughly. Gradually add the remaining water as you
knead the dough in the bowl, working it until it is elastic
and smooth and no longer sticks to your fingers, about 15
minutes. Rub a little oil over the top of the dough and
cover the bowl with a kitchen towel. Leave in a warm place
until doubled in size, about 2 hours.

Punch the dough down and knead again for a few minutes to make it uniformly smooth. Cut the dough into 12
equal pieces, then shape the pieces into 12 balls. Roll each
ball on a floured surface into circles about ¼ inch thick
and 6 or 7 inches in diameter. Dust lightly with flour and
cover with kitchen towels again, allowing them to rise for
45 minutes to 1 hour. Meanwhile, preheat the oven to 500°
and oil 2 large baking sheets.

Bake the bread for 5 to 7 minutes until the bottom is
lightly browned, then turn on the broiler and broil the
tops for about 30 seconds or until lightly browned.
Remove from the oven and wrap in the towel until serving.
MAKES 12

Cole Slaw

The lowcountry has as many recipes for cole slaw as it does for shrimp. This one, with no mayonnaise, can be made well in advance. It will keep for a long time and should be made at least twenty-four hours before you plan to serve it. Serve the slaw with a slotted spoon to drain off the liquid. If you want it to include mayonnaise or other seasonings, add them just before serving. It's delicious as is.

1½ cups water
1½ cups white vinegar
1 cup sugar
1 head of green cabbage (2 to 3 pounds), grated
2 medium red onions, finely chopped
1 bell pepper, finely chopped
1 carrot, peeled and grated
1 tablespoon salt
1 tablespoon mustard seed

Bring the water, vinegar, and sugar to a boil in a saucepan, then set aside to cool. Pour over the remaining ingredients, mix well, and refrigerate for at least 24 hours before serving.
SERVES 12

OPPOSITE: **The tabby foundation of the house.** LEFT: **The outdoor table set with the feast.** ABOVE: **The ruins of the nearby Chapel of Ease, made of tabby.**

Scuppernong Pie

Wild purple muscadines and tawny scuppernongs entwine among the hardwoods and pines throughout the South. Like Concords, they are native American "slip-skin" grapes that are available at farmers' markets and grocers throughout the country during their ephemeral season. If you can't find scuppernongs, use any of the native American grapes. If you use Concords, add a little lemon zest and juice for flavor.

1 pound (about 4 cups) unbleached all-purpose flour
Salt
1 cup sugar
¼ pound (1 stick) chilled unsalted butter
½ cup ice water
4 cups (about 2 pounds) slip-skin grapes
½ tablespoon cornstarch
1 tablespoon milk or half-and-half

To make the crust, sift the flour with a pinch of salt and 1 tablespoon of the sugar into a large mixing bowl. Cut the butter into the flour with a pastry blender or 2 knives until it is uniformly incorporated and there are no large clumps. Using a large metal slotted spoon, lift up spoonfuls of the mixture from the bottom of the bowl as you dribble the ice water into the bowl. Continue lifting up the mixture and sprinkling the water, stopping the moment you feel that the dough will hold together in a ball. Now grab the dough in your hands and gently push it all together into a ball. Wrap the dough in plastic wrap and put in the refrigerator while you make the filling.

Pulp the grapes by squeezing them over a nonreactive pot, allowing the seed-filled flesh to fall into the pot. Reserve the skins. Cook the pulp over medium-high heat just long enough to loosen the seeds, about 5 minutes, then press the pulp through a colander to remove the seeds. Combine the pulp with the skins, ¾ cup of the sugar, and the cornstarch, stirring well. Preheat the oven to 450° and place the rack in the center of the oven.

Remove the dough from the refrigerator and place on a lightly floured surface. Roll it out evenly to a thickness of about ⅛ inch. Place a 9-inch pie plate on top of the dough and cut out a circle large enough to fill it—a circle about 11 inches in diameter. Set the pie plate aside and roll the circle back up on the rolling pin, then gently lay it in the pan. Press it lightly into place, allowing the excess dough to hang over the sides. Fill with the fruit mixture.

Cut the remaining dough into long strips and gently make a lattice top on the pie. Run a sharp knife blade at an angle around the rim of the pie plate, cutting off excess dough. Lightly pinch the edge of dough all around the pie to seal it. Brush the crust with the milk or half-and-half, then sprinkle with some of the remaining sugar.

Place the pie in the oven and bake for 10 minutes. Lower the heat to 350° and bake for another 30 minutes or so, until the dough is richly golden brown all over. Allow to cool to lukewarm and serve without cream, which masks the distinctive flavor.

SERVES 8 TO 10

Red Velvet Cake

Deeply colored with cocoa and red food coloring, this cake is a year-round favorite. Though often served with a cream cheese icing, this old-fashioned shiny white "Noxema" frosting is preferred in the lowcountry. Don't laugh; it's delicious.

For the cake

¼ pound (1 stick) unsalted butter at room temperature

1½ cups sugar

2 eggs

¼ cup (2 ounces) red food coloring

2 tablespoons cocoa

2½ cups soft southern flour (see Sources) or cake flour

1 teaspoon salt

1 cup buttermilk at room temperature

1 teaspoon vanilla extract

1 tablespoon white vinegar

1 teaspoon baking soda

For the icing and assembly

5 tablespoons flour

1 cup milk

1 cup (2 sticks) unsalted butter at room temperature

1 cup sugar

1 teaspoon vanilla extract

To make the cake, preheat the oven to 350°. Grease and flour three 8-inch round cake pans.

Cream the butter and sugar in the large bowl of an electric mixer until fluffy. Add the eggs, one at a time, and beat well after each. Make a paste of the food coloring and cocoa and add to the mixture. Sift the flour and salt together into the mixture a little at a time, alternating with the buttermilk. Add the vanilla and blend well. Add the vinegar and soda, mix in well, then divide the batter among the 3 prepared pans. Bake for about 30 minutes or until a toothpick stuck into the center of the cake comes out clean. Cool on racks while you make the icing.

To make the icing, mix the flour and milk in the top of a double boiler and cook over simmering water until it is just thick, about 10 minutes. Remove from the heat and allow to cool completely. Cream the butter, sugar, and vanilla until very light and fluffy, about 10 minutes. Add to the flour mixture and beat until just mixed. Assemble the cake, with a thin layer of icing between the layers and covering the cake.

SERVES 12

OPPOSITE: **Fresh local scuppernong grapes.** BELOW: **Red velvet cake.**

SHRIMP, CRAB, AND OYSTERS

THE FLAT BROAD stretches of salt marsh that describe the coastline of the lowcountry are among the world's richest lands. Through meandering estuaries, creeks, and rivers, the spawn of untold thousands of life-forms are nourished amid the grasses and mud banks, continually washed by the ebb and flow of an eight-foot tide. Growing up on a boat, I more often than not pulled our meals from those waters — trolling for sea trout; gigging flounder; taking eels, flounder, and crabs from the trap; or walking carefully across the pluff mud at low tide to rake oysters and clams from their beds.

I also learned to throw a circular cast net for mullet and shrimp. Back then, those nets were hand-tied of cotton line by local fishermen, descendants of the slaves who had once worked the cotton plantations on the subtropical barrier islands that protect our inland cities. Perhaps no one enjoys more freedom than the men who work the waters of the lowcountry. Though saddled to the whims of nature, biting winds, and a fickle economy, the shrimpers, crabbers, and oystermen of our coast share a monklike devotion to their work and a serenity that only a life on the sea can bring.

BELOW: **Shrimp boats on the Georgia coast.**

To know the cuisine of the lowcounty is to know shellfish. Sephardic Jews, who early on came to Charleston — for more than one hundred years the country's largest Jewish settlement — ignored their dietary laws here where shellfish were so abundant; escabeche was made with shrimp and oysters. English, German, and French colonists, with a taste for sausages, ground oysters into their meat patties, then came to prefer them that way. And the Scots-Irish, with their taste for creamy seafood stews, boiled rice in milk, adding the meat and roe of female crabs, creating a lowcountry classic. Fresh, local food is the very heart of any cuisine. Shrimp, oysters, and crab remain

the preferred lowcountry foods.

In fall and winter—the "r" months—oysters are pulled from their natural beds on the South Carolina and Georgia coasts. The oysters are wild, not cultivated. They grow in clusters on the banks of the sinuous brackish creeks that flow in and out of those marshlands. Our oysters are meaty, juicy, and salty. They are perhaps best eaten raw, ungarnished, on the half shell, but the ritual oyster roast is a favored evening event throughout the cooler months. A roaring fire is built on the ground. Over it, a sheet of metal is placed, balanced on concrete blocks. Quickly rinsed of mud, the oysters are placed on the metal, then covered with a burlap bag soaked in water. Most locals don't allow the oysters to cook too long—just enough to warm them through and to loosen their hinges, so that the tangy liquor, tasting every bit of the ocean, doesn't escape.

Crabs are so plentiful that there is no license required or limits imposed for those taken on handlines, in dip nets or drop nets; residents may also have two crab pots per family. Boiled, steamed, or stewed, Atlantic blue crabs are among the sweetest fruits of the sea. Our classic she-crab soup is justly world renowned, and crab and shrimp boils, served on newspaper-covered tables, are common throughout all but the coldest months.

The shrimp run from as soon as the water warms in May until it first cools, around Thanksgiving. Trawlers hug the shores to pull them in for sale. The shrimping business is one of the lowcountry's most prosperous, but many sandlappers, as we call ourselves, prefer to cast for their own. They are put up in olive oil, served over grits and rice, are ground into pastes to spread on crackers as appetizers, or are simply dumped in pots of seasoned boiling water for a few moments and eaten with gusto. Most lowcountry freezers hold shrimp to last through the winter. A day need not necessarily include shrimp, crab, or oysters, but we don't go a week without.

ABOVE: **Feisty blue crabs.** BELOW: **Oyster beds at low tide.**

Autumn Dinner at Tabby Manse

Above: **The front portico of the house, overlooking the bay.** Opposite: **One of the twin dining rooms set for dinner.**

✛

Poached Fish with Ginger and
Lemon Thyme

Slow-Roast Rosemary Pork
with Pear Relish

Oven-Roasted Beets and Carrots
with Fresh Mint

Scalloped Turnips

Persimmon Pudding

✛

T ABBY WAS AN EARLY concretelike construction material made by mixing
oyster shells and sand with lime obtained
from burned shells. With its two-foot-thick
exterior walls composed entirely of tabby,
this celebrated Beaufort home commands
an unparalleled view of the wide bend in
the Beaufort River known as the Bay. Built
as a gift to his bride in 1786 by the success-
ful planter Thomas Fuller, Tabby Manse has changed family hands only
three times in its two-hundred-year history. Planned according to fashionable English and Palladian ideals, its massive, symmetrical eight
rooms mirror each other across the grand entrance hall. The delicate
double portico and sweeping stuccoed exterior stair lighten the approach
and welcome the visitor to its pine- and cypress-paneled rooms.
Operated as a guest house for one hundred years, it has been fully

restored by its current owners, who have added gardens and a modern kitchen to the rear of the house.

This formal autumn dinner begins with fish poached in white wine. The recipe dates from sixteenth-century England; it is adapted from *Martha Washington's Booke of Cookery*. The main course is pork roasted slowly with rosemary plucked from the garden—a sort

of Italian barbecue; pear relish (see Condiments) garnishes the meat. It is served with fall root vegetables—oven-roasted beets and carrots as well as scalloped turnips. Dessert is the lowcountry classic, persimmon pudding. Serve a medium-dry white such as a Vin de Pays d'Oc or a Marsanne with this meal, which should be enjoyed at a leisurely pace.

Poached Fish with Ginger and Lemon Thyme

This recipe varies little from one that appeared in *Martha Washington's Booke of Cookery*, annotated by the culinary historian Karen Hess. You can use any fish you like; just don't overcook it or let the liquid boil. I like to use sea trout (the southern form of weakfish), as we did here; the skin is thin and delicious. Buy whole fish, have the fishmonger fillet them for you, then bring the head and backbone home to make a stock to flavor the dish. Simply place the head and bones (with no blood, guts, or gills) in a saucepan, cover with water, add some onion, carrot, celery, and a few herbs, and allow to simmer for about 15 minutes, skimming any scum that rises to the surface. Add a little dry white wine and continue simmering for another 15 minutes, then strain out the solids and discard.

2 cups fish stock (see above)
½ cup dry white wine
A 1-inch piece of fresh gingerroot, peeled and sliced
6 sprigs of fresh lemon thyme
1 shallot, chopped
2 tablespoons unsalted butter at room temperature
4 fish fillets (2 pounds), with skins if delicate
Salt and freshly ground black pepper

Preheat the oven to its lowest setting and place 4 plates in it to warm.

Place the stock, wine, ginger, 2 sprigs of lemon thyme, the shallot, and the butter in a heavy wide sauté pan over high heat. Bring just to a boil. Season the fish with salt and pepper.

As soon as the liquid boils, lower the heat and place the fish flesh side down on the ginger and thyme sprigs. Cover the pan and cook at a bare simmer for about 4 minutes, then carefully turn the fillets over and continue to cook, covered, until the flesh is opaque and just flakes when pried, another 3 to 5 minutes, depending on the thickness of the fillets. Carefully lift the fish out of the liquid onto the warmed plates, returning them to the oven to keep them warm.

Increase the heat to high and reduce the liquid to a thick sauce. Strain and pour over the poached fish, garnishing each plate with a sprig of lemon thyme.
SERVES 4

OPPOSITE: **Looking out of the unpainted cypress drawing room**, TOP. **Copper pots in the kitchen**, BOTTOM.
ABOVE: **Poached fish on Dresden china.**

Slow-Roast Rosemary Pork with Pear Relish

This oven-roasted pork marries the southern idea of slow cooking with bold Mediterranean flavors taking the place of hickory smoke. The pear relish is the perfect sweet-and-sour condiment for the meat, which can be cooked in advance and reheated.

A 3- to 4-pound pork shoulder roast (a Boston butt)
Several sprigs of fresh rosemary
Kitchen twine
8 to 10 garlic cloves, halved

Preheat the oven to 250°.

Remove the blade from the shoulder: with the fatty side of the meat down, locate the straight line of the blade. Slice into the meat with a knife flush against the bone, following its contours. Lift the flesh away from the bone as it is cut free. Pull out the bone and stick a sprig of rosemary in the cavity. Tie the shoulder into a roll, with 2 or 3 more rosemary sprigs attached to the meat. Poke holes in the meat at 3-inch intervals and fill them with halved garlic cloves.

Place the meat fat side up on a rack in a roasting pan and place in the oven. Do not open the oven for several hours. It will take the meat at least 1 hour, and as much as 2, per pound to cook. It is done when it reaches 160°. The slowly rendered fat will drip through the meat, tenderizing as it imbues flavor. Remove from the oven and allow to rest for at least 20 minutes, then pull the tender meat into pieces. Discard excess fat if there is any. Serve the meat warm with pear relish.

SERVES 4

Oven-Roasted Beets and Carrots with Fresh Mint

This recipe, too, is rooted in the Mediterranean. You can roast the vegetables while the meat is cooking. Doneness of the vegetables, not the temperature of the oven, is what's important here.

4 large carrots
4 medium beets
Olive oil
Salt and freshly ground black pepper
Balsamic vinegar
Fresh mint

Scrub the carrots and beets well and place them in a roasting pan. Drizzle a little oil over the vegetables and season them with salt and pepper. Toss well, then place in a warm to moderate oven. Roast until the vegetables just barely give to the touch, or until they are cooked *al dente*; the beets will probably take longer than the carrots. If you are cooking the vegetables at 250° with the meat, they will take about 2 hours. Place them on a cutting board and cut the carrots into bite-size pieces. Peel the beets and discard the skins, then cut them bite size as well. Splash with a little balsamic vinegar, add a few mint leaves, and serve at room temperature.
SERVES 4

Scalloped Turnips

Serve this dish to those who think they don't like turnip roots, and you'll turn them into turnip lovers. They are made just like scalloped potatoes.

5 cups peeled and thinly sliced turnip roots (about
    5 medium turnips weighing about 2 pounds)
1 cup thinly sliced onions
3 tablespoons all-purpose flour
1 teaspoon salt
Freshly ground black pepper
2 tablespoons unsalted butter, cut into small dice
1½ cups scalded milk

Preheat the oven to 375°.

Place a layer of turnips in a 2-quart greased casserole dish. Make a thin layer of onion rings, then sprinkle a little of the flour and salt and pepper on the layer. Place a few dice of butter on the layer, then repeat the process until the dish is filled with the turnips. Slowly pour the scalded milk into the dish and cover the dish tightly with a lid or aluminum foil. Bake for 45 minutes.

Remove the lid and bake for another 15 minutes. If not browned on the top, you can run the dish under the broiler for a moment if desired.
SERVES 4 TO 6

OPPOSITE: **Slow-roast pork, oven-roasted beets and carrots, and scalloped turnips are served with pear relish.** LEFT: **A wall panel is removed to expose the tabby construction.**

Persimmon Pudding

If you have access to native American persimmons, by all means use them; their flavor is incomparable. Serve this old-fashioned dessert with mounds of crème fraîche, a substitute for which you can make a day in advance.

For the crème fraîche
1 cup heavy cream
½ cup sour cream
1½ teaspoons fresh lemon juice

For the pudding
¼ pound (1 stick) unsalted butter
1 cup sugar
2 eggs
2 pounds persimmons
½ teaspoon salt
1 teaspoon baking soda
1½ cups all-purpose flour

To make the crème fraîche, mix the cream and sour cream together in a bowl. Allow to sit at room temperature for 6 to 8 hours. Place a coffee filter in a funnel or line a fine sieve with paper towels, add the cream, and set aside to drain for 2 to 3 hours, until thick.

Mix in the lemon juice and store in the refrigerator for up to 1 week.

To make the pudding, preheat the oven to 350°. Grease a 2-quart Bundt pan.

Cream the butter and sugar together until fluffy, then add the eggs, one at a time, beating well after each.

Press the persimmons through a nonaluminum colander; you should have about 2 cups of pulp. Add the pulp to the butter and egg mixture, then sift the dry ingredients into the bowl, mixing all well together. Spoon the batter into the pan and bake for about 1 hour, or until the pudding is golden brown on top and it just begins to pull from the sides of the pan.

Serve warm or at room temperature.
SERVES 4 TO 6

RIGHT: **Pomegranates, persimmons, and wildflowers.**
FAR RIGHT: **Persimmon pudding with crème fraîche.**

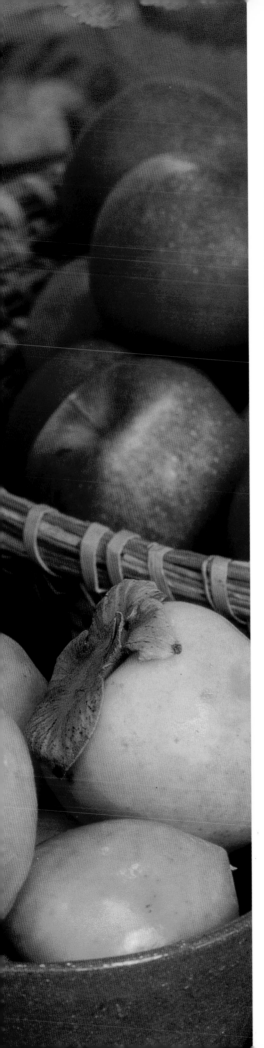

Burgundy Tasting and Candlelight Dinner at the Elizabeth Barnwell Gough House

ABOVE: **The front portico of the house.**
OPPOSITE: **Late eighteenth- and early nineteenth-century Anglo-Irish wine glasses and rinsers.**

✛

Shrimp Consommé

Rabbit Braised in
White Wine with Tomatoes

Turnip Greens

Potato Croquettes

Baked Orange Custard with
Cranberry Glaze

✛

THOUGH OFTEN CALLED a twin to the slightly older Tabby Manse, the Gough house of 1789 sits on a large city block, several blocks from the water, and is surrounded by a high wall enclosing both formal and informal English-style gardens. A large arched Venetian window looks onto a rear gallery, and the staircase arcs gracefully in the joyous central hall, bright with Georgian colors. The front portico reflects the beginning of Adamesque restraint, and the stuccoed tabby walls are scored to resemble stone.

An enviable collection of Georgian and Federal antiques is perfectly suited to the home's magnificent style. This late afternoon fall tasting is of just-released Burgundys; in the Federal era, the wine tasted probably would have been claret.

The tasting segues into a candlelight dinner of shrimp consommé, rabbit braised with white wine and tomatoes, and baked orange custard with a cranberry glaze. The table is one of a set made in London for the Duke of Manchester on his appointment as Governor of Jamaica in 1807. Water is served in silver julep cups. The biggest of the white Burgundys (Chardonnay) tasted should continue to be served with this autumn dinner.

For the stock

1 pound extremely fresh heads-on
    shrimp, or ½ pound shrimp plus
    ½ pound lobster, crab, or
    crawfish shells
1 carrot
1 celery rib
A few fresh herbs, such as thyme,
    parsley, basil, oregano, and savory
1 small onion, unpeeled and halved
1½ quarts water

For the consommé

1 small hot pepper such as a jalapeño,
    seeded and thinly sliced, to taste
A 1-inch piece of fresh gingerroot,
    peeled
1 small carrot, peeled and finely
    julienned
2 to 3 scallions, cut both in slivers
    and slices
Salt
Cilantro leaves

To make the stock, remove the heads
and shells from the shrimp, dropping
them into a nonreactive stockpot.
Cover the shrimp well and place in
the refrigerator.

Add the rest of the ingredients to
the pot and cook at a low boil, uncovered, for about 45 minutes, skimming
any scum that rises to the surface.
The liquid should have reduced by a
third. Strain out the solids and
discard.

To make the consommé, warm the
stock over medium heat, adding the
reserved shrimp, the pepper, ginger,
carrot, and scallions. Do not allow to boil. Remove from
the heat when the shrimp are just shy of being cooked, no
more than 5 minutes. Season to taste with salt, then divide
among 4 warmed bowls. Garnish with cilantro leaves and
serve immediately.

SERVES 4

Shrimp Consommé

This clear, spicy soup is a touch of the Orient in the lowcountry. Here, we keep shrimp stock on hand in the
freezer. If you don't live where you can get freshly caught,
heads-on shrimp, make the stock with shrimp shells,
adding some crab, crawfish, or lobster shells to make up for
the missing heads. Whenever you cook crustaceans, place
the shells in a plastic bag in the freezer, then when you
have enough you can make a stock.

ABOVE: **Shrimp consommé is eaten with rare Scottish soup
spoons from 1759. Water is poured in julep cups.**

Rabbit Braised in White Wine with Tomatoes

Rabbit is a much overlooked food that deserves to be cooked more often. In this light, braised dish, the white meat falls off the bone.

2 rabbits (2 pounds each), fresh or defrosted frozen, cut into quarters, rinsed, and patted dry

Salt and freshly ground black pepper

1 teaspoon mixed dried herbs, such as herbes de Provence or Italian seasoning, ground

¼ cup all-purpose flour

¼ cup olive oil

1 cup chopped onions

2 cups peeled and chopped vine-ripened tomatoes, or 1 14½-ounce can whole tomatoes, chopped, with their juice

2 cups chicken stock

2 cups dry white wine

Season the rabbits with salt and pepper. Mix the herbs and flour together in a shallow bowl and dredge the rabbit in it, shaking off any excess. Heat the oil in a Dutch oven over medium-high heat and brown the rabbit pieces all over, removing them from the pot as they are done. Set aside.

Add the onions and sauté until they become transparent, 5 to 10 minutes. Add the tomatoes and cook until the juice has evaporated, another 5 to 10 minutes. Add the stock and the wine and bring to a boil, scraping up any pieces that may have stuck to the bottom of the pan. Add the rabbit, lower the heat, and simmer, covered, until tender, about 1 hour. Serve immediately, napping the rabbit pieces with the sauce. If the sauce isn't thick, remove the pieces to a serving platter and reduce over high heat until it reaches the desired consistency. Pour over the rabbit or serve in a gravy boat.

SERVES 4 TO 6

Turnip Greens

Most Southerners adore greens, but it is a misconception that we cook greens to death. All greens are cooked until tender. Collards may take as long as two hours, but tender young turnip greens should be done in about thirty minutes. Greens are traditionally served with a cruet of hot pepper vinegar (see Condiments).

1 small piece of smoked ham hock (about ¼ pound)
A bunch of young turnip greens (about 2 pounds)

Place the hock in a stockpot and cover with 3 or 4 inches of water. Cook at a low boil about 30 minutes until the water is pleasantly infused with flavor. In the meantime, clean the greens by placing them in a sink filled with cold water. Shake them around in the water to loosen any sand or grit and repeat until they are thoroughly cleaned.

Cut any tough stems from the greens and discard, along with any yellowed or blemished leaves. Tear the leaves into several pieces and add them to the pot. Reduce the heat and simmer uncovered until they are tender, or to taste.

SERVES 4 TO 6

Potato Croquettes

These fritters can be made while the rest of the dinner is cooking. You can set an oven to its lowest setting and place the fritters on racks in the oven to stay warm.

1½ pounds potatoes, boiled and peeled
Salt and freshly ground black pepper
1 shallot, minced
1 tablespoon chopped mixed fresh herbs, to include mint,
    thyme, and parsley
2 eggs
4 tablespoons (½ stick) unsalted butter
1 cup dry bread crumbs

Mash the potatoes in a large mixing bowl or run them through a ricer or food mill into the bowl. Season them with salt and pepper. Add the shallot, herbs, and one of the eggs and mix well. Place the mixture in the refrigerator to chill for 30 minutes.

Place a wire rack on a baking sheet and turn the oven to its lowest setting. Begin heating the butter over medium-high heat in a sauté pan.

Place the bread crumbs in a shallow bowl. Beat the remaining egg in a small bowl. Remove the potato mixture from the refrigerator and, with moist hands, form little tubes of the mixture about the size of 2 fingers. Dip the croquettes in the egg, then in the bread crumbs. Fry in hot butter until golden brown all over, about a minute or so on each side. Remove the fritters to the prepared baking sheet to keep warm or serve immediately.

MAKES 16 CROQUETTES

OPPOSITE: **The exuberant staircase.**
LEFT: **Braised rabbit, turnip greens, and potato croquettes.**

FAR LEFT: A late eighteenth-century Venetian lamp hangs in the stairwell overlooking the rear gallery. LEFT: Rare Central and South American prints in the library. TOP: An American Federal sofa draped with Damascus silk from the 1920s. ABOVE: A bust in the library.

Baked Orange Custard with Cranberry Glaze

You'll need to prepare this dish several hours before serving so that it has time to chill.

For the glaze and garnish

1 large, juicy orange

1½ cups cranberries (about ½ pound), plus a few extra for garnish

½ cup sugar

For the pudding

2¼ cups milk

2 teaspoons unsalted butter, plus butter for greasing the ramekins

3 eggs

¼ cup sugar

¼ teaspoon salt

To make the glaze, grate a teaspoon of orange zest and set aside. Cut strips of zest for the garnish and set aside. Squeeze ½ cup of juice into a saucepan, add the cranberries and sugar, and bring to a boil over high heat, stirring constantly. When all of the berries have split open and the liquid has reduced by a fourth, remove from the heat and press the mixture through a fine sieve. Set aside to cool.

To make the pudding, preheat the oven to 300° and put a pot of water on to boil.

Scald the milk. While the milk is scalding, butter four 4-ounce ramekins. Refrigerate the ramekins to chill the butter, then grease again.

Beat the eggs until fluffy. Cream 2 teaspoons of butter with the sugar and salt, add to the eggs, and beat until thick and lemony. Add the teaspoon of reserved orange zest and the scalded milk and beat in well. Strain the mixture into the greased cups, filling them to ½ inch from the rim. Place in a baking pan and fill the pan with hot water. Bake the custards for 1 hour or until a knife poked in the center comes out clean. Remove the custards from the water bath and set aside to cool, then chill until serving.

To serve, pour a pool of sauce on each of 4 dessert plates. Dip the ramekins in very hot water to melt the butter and loosen the puddings. Invert each pudding onto a plate, then drizzle a little more glaze onto each. Roughly chop the reserved cranberries and scatter them and the reserved orange zest on the puddings for garnish.

SERVES 4

OPPOSITE: **Orange custard with a cranberry orange sauce.** ABOVE: **A late eighteenth-century mahogany, satinwood, and boxwood spoon urn.**

Easter Sunday at Riverview

ABOVE: **Spring flowers from the garden.**
OPPOSITE: **The stupendous river view, with the dock stretching over marsh grass and oyster beds.**

✠

Rockefeller Turnovers
Rack of Lamb
Fresh Asparagus
Barley and Wild Rice
Greek Cookies

✠

O NE OF BEAUFORT'S oldest homes, Riverview lies on the eastern peninsula of the city heavily shaded by live oaks and surrounded by salt marshes. Its broad double piazzas on the southern exposure are original to the house; they provide shade and catch the subtropical breezes as they overlook a gated front lawn planted with indigenous and imported plant specimens.

The house is relatively small, but charming and comfortable due to the large amount of beautiful, modest woodwork and the windows in every room, six over nine lights, many with the original glass. This Easter dinner reflects the owner's Greek heritage. Serve the oyster-filled turnovers with drinks before dinner, then serve a big, tannic red wine such as an aged St. Estèphe or Chianti Classico with the lamb. Port is served with the cookies.

Rockefeller Turnovers

I developed these appetizers for *Food & Wine* magazine. The ingredients for Oysters Rockefeller are chopped together, tucked into puff pastry turnovers, and baked. They can be assembled ahead of time, refrigerated, and baked when you're ready to eat. Serve them warm before dinner with drinks.

½ pint shucked oysters
1 sheet frozen puff pastry
4 tablespoons (½ stick) unsalted butter
¼ cup finely chopped celery
1 shallot, minced
1 garlic clove, minced
½ pound spinach, trimmed, chopped, steamed, and
    drained, or ½ of a 10-ounce package of frozen chopped
    spinach, thawed and drained
½ teaspoon salt
A few drops of Tabasco or a pinch of cayenne, to taste
2 tablespoons fresh lemon juice
2 tablespoons Herbsaint or Pernod (anise-flavored
    liquors), or ¼ teaspoon ground anise seeds
¼ cup fine, dry bread crumbs
1 tablespoon chopped anchovy fillets
1 egg

At least an hour before serving, place the oysters in a sieve over a bowl in the refrigerator to thoroughly drain. Remove the puff pastry from the freezer and allow to thaw at room temperature for 20 minutes.

Melt the butter in a skillet over medium heat, then sauté the celery and shallot until they are translucent, about 5 minutes. Add the garlic, spinach, and salt and stir well to combine. Add the Tabasco or cayenne, the lemon juice, and anise flavoring and continue cooking until most of the liquid has cooked out of the spinach and it has reduced to a puree, about another 5 minutes. Remove from the heat, fold in the bread crumbs, and place the mixture on a plate to cool.

Remove the oysters from the refrigerator and place on a cutting board with the anchovies. Finely chop the oysters and anchovies together. Fold into the spinach mixture, then place again in the sieve to drain.

Roll out the sheet of puff pastry on a very lightly floured surface into a 14-inch square. Cut the square into sixteen 3½-inch squares, then place a tablespoon of the mixture in the center of each square. Lightly moisten two adjacent edges of the pastry with water, then fold into triangular turnovers, corner to corner. Crimp the edges together with the tines of a fork and place the turnovers on a baking sheet.

Make a wash by beating the egg with 2 tablespoons of water. Lightly brush the top of each turnover with the wash, not letting any drip down the sides. Refrigerate until ready to bake.

Preheat the oven to 400°.

Remove the baking sheet from the refrigerator and, just before baking, lightly brush the tops of the turnovers with the egg wash again. Bake for 20 minutes, or until golden brown. Serve hot.

MAKES 16 TURNOVERS

RIGHT: **Oyster- and spinach-filled puff pastry appetizers.** OPPOSITE: **The table set for dinner, with camellias.**

Rack of Lamb

This simple preparation is an Easter classic. Fresh herbs from the garden add flavor in the oven and color on the plate. Have the butcher french-cut the racks for you, leaving the rib bones pristine.

2 frenched 8-rib racks of lamb
Freshly ground black pepper
8 to 10 garlic cloves, peeled
2 tablespoons fresh parsley
2 tablespoons fresh rosemary, plus some for garnish
1 tablespoon fine dry bread crumbs

Place the meat in a roasting pan, fat side up, and season it with black pepper. Allow it to come to room temperature. Preheat the oven to 450°.

Place the garlic and herbs on a cutting board and chop them well together. Add the garlic mixture to the bread crumbs and mix well. Rub the mixture all over the racks, then place in the preheated oven. Bake for 10 minutes at 450°, lower the heat to 425°, and bake for an additional 20 to 30 minutes, depending on the degree of doneness you desire. Allow to rest for 5 minutes before slicing 2 or 3 chops per person and serving on warmed plates.
SERVES 6

Fresh Asparagus

For 6 people, you'll need 2 pounds of asparagus. One of the easiest ways to cook it is in a microwave: simply place the asparagus in a Pyrex roasting pan, cover with plastic wrap, and cook on high at 2-minute intervals. When the asparagus is done, drizzle with some extra-virgin olive oil and season with a little salt and pepper. If you're cooking it well before you serve it, cook it until it is slightly underdone, then remove the asparagus from the pan and spread the stalks out on a kitchen towel so that they don't continue to cook. You can also run cold water over them to stop the cooking, then reheat them just before serving.

RIGHT: **Rack of lamb, asparagus, and barley with wild rice.**

LEFT: **The house with front and back doors open to allow sea breezes to flow completely through the house.** ABOVE: **The staircase and a warden's closet in the rear parlor.** BELOW: **Rosemary in the parterre.**

Barley and Wild Rice

This combination of grains provides earthy flavors and a contrast of textures to this lamb dinner. Serve it with roast meats, poultry, or game.

8 cups water
1 teaspoon salt
1½ cups medium barley
½ cup wild rice

Bring the water to a boil in a large saucepan. Add the salt, barley, and wild rice. Cover, reduce heat, and simmer for about 45 minutes, or until the barley is tender and the water has been absorbed. Remove from the heat and allow to stand for at least 5 minutes before serving.
SERVES 6

Greek Cookies

The recipe for these irresistible cookies made with olive oil was adapted from *Popular Greek Recipes*, published by the Greek Ladies Philoptochos Society in Charleston in 1957. They have a delicate crumb and are not too sweet. Serve them with a glass of port. The dough can be refrigerated for several weeks in an airtight plastic bag and baked at a later date.

1 orange
1 cup olive oil
2 cups sugar, plus 3 tablespoons
2 eggs
½ teaspoon baking soda
2 teaspoons baking powder
3½ to 4 cups sifted all-purpose flour
2 cups water
1 teaspoon ground cinnamon

Grate the zest of the orange and set aside. Juice the orange, adding the juice to the zest.

Beat the oil and 1 cup of the sugar together well, then add the eggs, one at a time, beating constantly. Dissolve the soda in the orange juice and add to the creamed mixture. Add the baking powder, then enough of the flour to make a soft, manageable dough.

Preheat the oven to 350° and grease 2 baking sheets.

Take small pieces of dough, about the size of a walnut, and shape each into a ball. Place the balls on a cookie sheet and flatten each one into a 2- to 3-inch cookie, ¼ to ⅜ inch thick. Bake for 20 to 25 minutes, or until they just begin to blush with color.

While the cookies are baking, combine 1 cup of sugar with the water in a small saucepan. Bring to a boil, then reduce the heat to low to keep the syrup warm. Mix the remaining 3 tablespoons of sugar with the cinnamon in a shallow bowl. Place in a sugar shaker if you have one.

When the cookies are done, remove them from the baking sheet to cool. Place wire racks over a baking sheet and, as the cookies cool, use tongs to dip each cookie quickly into the syrup. Place on the racks and sprinkle with cinnamon sugar.
MAKES ABOUT 50 COOKIES

BELOW: **The cookies are made with olive oil and are served with port in custom-made German glasses.**

LEFT: **Bone-handled English service-ware.** BELOW: **A lamp and orchid in the hallway, whose walls are single planks.**

Lunch on the Veranda of the Secession House

✦

Tomato Bouillon

Icebox Rolls

Alligator Pear and Crabmeat Salad

Peach Cobbler

✦

ABOVE: **Dainty Mary Corcoran azaleas in a Masons vase adorn the table on the porch.** OPPOSITE: **Even the rear gate is handsomely detailed.**

PERHAPS NO HOUSE better illustrates Beaufort's peculiar history than this one built by Milton Maxcy in 1813. Maxcy had come from Massachusetts to open a school for boys; he built his imposing home overlooking the bay on the tabby foundations of an early eighteenth-century house. When Edmund Rhett acquired the home, he remodeled it in the popular Greek Revival fashion, with a double portico supported by an arched stuccoed basement (painted pink, I think, to resemble coral). Ionic columns support the first-story portico; Corinthian, the second. A handsome marble staircase with ornate ironwork on the eastern exposure forms an imposing entrance to the home, which sits on a full city block. There are extant outbuildings, including the kitchen, and a vast garden. The interior boasts some

of the finest plaster moldings in the lowcountry, large airy rooms, and full-length windows that open onto the inviting verandas, where this simple lunch of tomato soup, crab and avocado salad, and peach cobbler is served.

Edmund Rhett's brother Robert was known as the Father of Secession; it was in this house that the Ordinance of Secession from the Union was drafted. Shortly after the renovations to the house were completed in 1861, thirty thousand Union troops invaded and occupied Beaufort as the Union headquarters in the South. Most of the white population left the city, never to return. The Rhetts were never able to enjoy the house as it is today. During the war, Secession House was used as both hospital and paymaster's office. In twentieth-century renovations, layers of paint were removed from the original plaster walls in the basement, revealing graffiti scribbled by Union soldiers.

RIGHT: **Ionic columns on the main floor veranda.** OPPOSITE: **Clear tomato soup.**

Tomato Bouillon

This is an elegant, thin tomato soup that is flavorful and bright, the perfect starter for a spring or summer meal. If you can't find vine-ripened tomatoes, use the best canned ones available.

1 cup chopped onion
½ cup finely chopped carrot
¼ cup finely chopped celery
¼ cup extra-virgin olive oil
5 cups vine-ripened tomatoes (about 3 pounds), cut into wedges, or 1 28-ounce can plus 1 14½-ounce can high-quality whole tomatoes
2½ tablespoons tomato paste
1 garlic clove, minced
1 teaspoon salt
1 sprig fresh cut thyme
Several parsley sprigs, plus a little extra for garnish
1 bay leaf
1 quart chicken stock
Freshly ground white pepper

Sauté the onion, carrot, and celery in the oil in a large nonreactive sauté pan over medium heat until the vegetables are soft, about 10 minutes. Add the tomatoes, tomato paste, garlic, salt, and herbs. Bring to a boil, reduce the heat, cover the pan, and allow to simmer for 20 minutes, stirring occasionally. Strain the mixture well.

Add the stock to the sauté pan, then add the strained tomato mixture. Simmer for another 15 minutes, then correct the seasoning with white pepper. Strain a second time for a clear texture, then serve warm, garnished with some chopped parsley.

SERVES 4 TO 6

Icebox Rolls

This old-fashioned roll must have been developed as the refrigerator—originally just iceboxes—became more common. Icebox rolls are sometimes made with mashed potatoes and nearly always with scalded milk or buttermilk. They also usually contain a lot of sugar; mine are not sweet.

These simple breads are also known as "stir and serve" rolls because they require no kneading. The dough will keep for several days under refrigeration; just use what you need and return it to the icebox for later use.

1 package active dry yeast
1 teaspoon sugar
½ cup warm water, 110° to 120°
6 to 7 cups all-purpose flour
1 tablespoon salt
¼ pound (1 stick) unsalted butter, melted and cooled
2 cups buttermilk at room temperature

Dissolve the yeast and sugar in the warm water. Leave in a warm place for about 10 minutes to proof; it should be slightly bubbly.

Sift 6 cups of the flour with the salt into a large warmed mixing bowl. Make a well in the center. Mix the butter and the buttermilk with the yeast mixture, then pour the liquid ingredients into the dry. Stir the mixture well with a wooden spoon until the dough is smooth and pulls away from the sides of the bowl. Add more of the sifted flour if necessary.

Push all of the dough together into a ball and place it in an oiled bowl, turning it to grease all sides. Cover the bowl tightly with plastic wrap and set aside to rise in a warm place for 1 hour. Punch down the dough and mix until smooth again. At this point you can cover the dough and refrigerate for up to 4 days or you can continue with the recipe.

When ready to bake, cut off as much of the dough as you need, returning the rest, covered, to the refrigerator. For dinner rolls, shape 2-inch pieces of dough with floured hands into 2-inch balls, then roll the balls between floured palms into 4-inch rolls. Place 1 or 2 inches apart on a greased baking sheet, cover with a damp tea towel, and allow to rise for about 30 minutes, or until nearly doubled in size.

Preheat the oven to 400° while the rolls are rising, then bake them until golden brown, about 15 minutes. Serve immediately.

MAKES 3 DOZEN ROLLS

LEFT AND ABOVE: **Graffiti in the basement drawn by Union soldiers during the Civil War.** BELOW: **The elegant marble-and-iron staircase.**

Alligator Pear and Crabmeat Salad

Avocados used to be called "alligator pears" in the low-country, a reference to their pebbly skins. Here they are served on a bed of greens, halved and filled with fresh lump crabmeat garnished with grapefruit and a little olive oil. Keep this salad simple, using the finest ingredients, and assemble it at the last possible moment.

1 pound mixed young salad greens
2 perfectly ripe avocados
2 grapefruits, one yellow and one pink or red, sectioned
1 pound fresh lump crabmeat, picked over for pieces of shell
4 scallions, slivered
1 ripe jalapeño pepper, seeded, stemmed, deribbed, and cut into small dice
Several fresh basil leaves, julienned
3/8 cup extra-virgin olive oil
2 lemons
Salt and freshly ground black pepper

Divide the salad greens among 4 plates. Halve the avocados and remove the pits, then place one avocado half on each plate of greens. Rub a piece of grapefruit section over the cut surfaces of the avocados to prevent them from coloring.

Fill each avocado half with crabmeat. Divide the grapefruit sections, scallions, jalapeño, and basil among the plates. Drizzle the oil over the salads, then drizzle the juice of one of the lemons over the salads. Quarter the other lemon and place a piece on each plate. Season with salt and pepper and serve immediately.
SERVES 4

Peach Cobbler

This is a favored southern dessert, often called "cup o', cup o', cup o'," for its simple batter of 1 cup milk, 1 cup sugar, and 1 cup flour. It is utter simplicity to make. Use perfect summer peaches, or, as we did for this spring-time luncheon, frozen ones. If you use frozen peaches, you can thaw them in a microwave, adding a little sugar and lemon juice to encourage juiciness.

You can serve this cobbler hot from the oven, warm, or at room temperature. Offer some heavy cream or crème fraîche with the dish.

¼ pound (1 stick) unsalted butter
2 to 4 cups peeled and sliced peaches with juice
1 cup sugar
2 teaspoons baking powder
1 cup all-purpose flour
1 cup milk

Put the butter in a 2-quart casserole dish, place in a cold oven, and preheat to 350°. If the peaches aren't juicy, sprinkle them with some of the sugar and set aside.

Sift the sugar, baking powder, and flour into a mixing bowl, add the milk, and mix until well blended. When the butter has melted and the oven has reached 350°, pour the batter evenly into the casserole. Add the peaches and their juice, distributing them evenly but keeping an outer edge of batter. Return to the oven and bake for about 1 hour, or until the top is golden brown.

SERVES 4 TO 8

OPPOSITE LEFT: **Crab and avocado salad with grapefruit.** ABOVE: **A view of the arched basement and first floor portico.** LEFT: **Peach cobbler, with heavy cream served from a nineteenth-century "Ribbon candy" pitcher.**

SAVANNAH

SAVANNAH WAS ESTABLISHED ON A high bluff on the southern bank of the river of the same name in 1733. Often called the best-planned city in America, it has continued to spread out from its original grid of small lots around twenty small parks, the shady squares that make Savannah also one of the most beautiful. Though the city suffered disastrous fires in the late eighteenth and early nineteenth centuries, enough of the early buildings survive that the city is a veritable museum of colonial, Federal, Greek Revival, and Victorian architecture.

Nowhere in America was a colony more closely tied to Georgian England; prevailing English tastes swept through the colony long after the Revolution. The architect William Jay brought fine English Regency style to the city and it flourished in both public and private buildings. Greek porticoes graced the brick and stone homes, raised on high basements opening onto sidewalks. Ironwork embellished balconies, balustrades, cornices, and door surrounds. Fine inlaid furniture was imported from England, mahogany came from the Caribbean, and local craftsmen began to excel in wood- and plasterwork.

If Charleston and Beaufort are defined by their piazzas and porticoes, Savannah is by her stoops. The raised stoop with exuberant cast iron is one of Savannah's unique features. Conrad Aiken wrote of "that wonderful stoop . . . which led to the second story, with its iron railing and brownstone steps, and the little door under it . . . was the real essence of the house, to begin with, . . . above the rich dark dirt of the street, and which, whether in sunlight or moonlight, kept forever a moving pattern of leaf-shadow turning and revolving over the serene housefront of tall windows and wrought-iron balconies, like an evanescent stencilling." Some streets of the city, with their massive row houses rising above the brick walkways, resemble a subtropical London. The live oaks in the squares have now grown enormous, forming canopies over the streets. Aiken called them his "first trees, the symbols therefore of all that was tree."

Monuments erected in the parks honor the city's heroes; they flush with rich greens in the humidity. Everywhere is the contrast of iron and flowers, heavy and light, sunshine and shade. Colonial clapboard abuts Georgian brick. Adam restraint is next-door neighbor to Gothic Revival. And the two-mile-square Historic District adjoins the enormous Victorian section, which boasts nearly a thousand late nineteenth- and early twentieth-century homes. Presented by General Sherman to President Lincoln as a Christmas present, Savannah was spared the torch of war. What survives is a graceful, vibrant city of beautiful homes, where entertaining at table has been at the very core of life for more than 250 years.

PRECEDING PAGES: A typical Savannah stoop might include many elements such as brick, wood, iron, and stone. OPPOSITE: Savannah ironwork. LEFT: The Polish-born Commander Pulaski was mortally wounded leading a cavalry defense in Savannah in 1779. The monument is in Pulaski Square. ABOVE: Savannah row houses.

OPPOSITE: **Iron and shadows on stucco walls.** ABOVE LEFT: **This turn-of-the-century development later became Ardsley Park along Victory Drive.** LEFT: **A double portico overlooking a downtown square.** ABOVE: **Savannah ironwork.**

Late Summer Dinner on Ardsley Park

ABOVE: **The formal drawing room features a pair of marble and gilt bronze Louis XVI candelabra.** OPPOSITE: **The dining room set for dinner.**

✛

Kir Royale

Blue Cheese and Pecan Wafers

Sautéed Veal Chops with
Oyster Mushrooms

Wilted Spinach

Mashed Sweet and White Potatoes
with Garlic Chives

Popovers

Chocolate Pots de Crème

✛

THIS SPACIOUS turn-of-the-century home was built off palmetto-lined Estill Avenue (later Victory Drive) in what was supposed to have become the "Atlantic Playground of the South," a Palm Beach–like suburb of Savannah now shaded by towering live oaks. Surrounded by an open veranda paved with Italian tile and a handsome balustrade and porte-cochere, the imposing Italianate home exudes a regal presence as it looks out over Ardsley Park. A greenhouse for the owner's orchids and a swimming pool flank the rear entrances.

Dinner begins with Kir Royale—a drink made by spiking champagne

with a little crème de cassis—and cocktail wafers made with blue cheese and pecans. Dinner is served on antique Spode; the pots au crème are Limoges. The dining room reflects the owner's eclectic collection that includes Regency furniture, Italian glass and pottery, Meissen porcelain, and a fine Czechoslovakian lead crystal chandelier. The candlelight dinner of sautéed veal is accompanied by fresh local mushrooms, spinach, and whipped sweet and white potatoes. Serve a big, white Burgundy such as a Meursault with the meal.

LEFT: **The facade of the house.**
ABOVE: **Orchids, an inlaid Regency linen press, and a Chippendale chair.**

Pinch off 1-inch pieces of the dough and roll them between your palms to form little balls. Flatten each ball into a circle about 1½ to 2 inches in diameter and place on baking sheets. Bake until golden brown, about 20 to 25 minutes.

MAKES ABOUT 3 DOZEN

Sautéed Veal Chops with Oyster Mushrooms

Ben Cramer's LowCountry Exotic Mushroom Farm (see Sources) produces beautiful shiitake, portobello, and oyster mushrooms about a half hour outside Charleston on idyllic John's Island. Encourage your grocer to carry fresh mushrooms. Most metropolitan areas now have growers such as Ben nearby to supply the growing demand for these so-called exotics. Try to find fresh oyster mushrooms with caps no bigger than 2 inches across for this dish.

2 tablespoons unsalted butter
2 tablespoons extra-virgin olive oil
6 bone-in veal rib chops, about ¾ inch thick and
    6 ounces each
Salt and freshly ground black pepper
1 pound fresh mushrooms, preferably oyster

Melt the butter with the oil in a very large sauté pan over medium-high heat, then add the chops. Sauté the chops until they are done to your liking (about 3 minutes per side for medium rare; twice that long for well done), seasoning them with salt and pepper. Remove them from the pan to a warmed platter.

Immediately dump all of the mushrooms at once into the pan, shaking it to loosen any little browned bits and to keep the mushrooms from sticking. Cook the mushrooms until they become limp and have lost most of their liquid, about 5 minutes. Season to taste with salt and pepper, then pour the mushrooms over the chops. Serve immediately.

SERVES 6

Blue Cheese and Pecan Wafers

These are easy to make and will keep for several days in an airtight container; frozen, they'll last even longer.

1¼ cups all-purpose flour
¾ teaspoon salt
4 tablespoons (½ stick) unsalted butter, softened
⅜ pound blue cheese, crumbled
½ cup chopped pecans

Preheat the oven to 350°. Sift together the flour and salt. Cream the butter and cheese together in a mixing bowl. Add the dry ingredients, then the nuts, and mix well. Don't worry if the dough seems too dry; work with it in your hands until it comes together in a ball.

ABOVE: **Blue cheese and pecan wafers are served with Kir Royale.**

ABOVE LEFT: **Sautéed veal chops with oyster mushrooms, wilted spinach, and mashed sweet and white potatoes are served with popovers. The tablecloth was handmade for the family in Korea.** LEFT: **Lady's slipper orchid with Toby jug, humidor, and lusterware pitcher.** ABOVE: **The mashed sweet and white potatoes are served in early nineteenth-century Davenport. The Meissen urn depicts equestrian scenes.**

Wilted Spinach

The lowcountry has long been renowned for the vast variety of greens that are grown here. In this recipe, spinach is wilted in a little olive oil at the very last minute.

2 tablespoons extra-virgin olive oil
2½ pounds fresh, cleaned spinach leaves
Fresh lemon juice, salt, and freshly ground black pepper

Just before serving, place a large Dutch oven over high heat and add the oil. Dump all of the spinach in at once, quickly stir-frying the greens. As soon as all of it is wilted, remove from the heat, season to taste with the lemon juice, salt, and pepper and serve immediately.
SERVES 6

Mashed Sweet and White Potatoes with Garlic Chives

Everyone loves this colorful and delicious alternative to mashed potatoes. Don't try to mash them with a blender or food processor; they'll turn to paste. If you can find garlic chives, use them to garnish and flavor this side dish.

2 to 3 large white baking potatoes
2 to 3 large white sweet potatoes
1½ cups whipping cream
Salt and freshly ground white pepper
Garlic chives for garnish

Preheat the oven to 375°. Scrub the potatoes well and prick the white potatoes in 2 or 3 places with a fork. Bake the potatoes until they give to the touch, about 45 minutes for the sweet potatoes, and 1 hour for the white. Bring the cream to a boil in a small saucepan, then turn off the heat.

Scoop the flesh out of the baked potatoes into a large mixing bowl and mash with a potato masher or by putting through a food mill. Beat the cream in a little at a time with a heavy wire whisk, seasoning with the salt and white pepper. Garnish with the garlic chives and serve immediately.
SERVES 6

Popovers

Popovers are an old lowcountry treat, often called "cream muffins" in the older cookbooks. This recipe works consistently well if you use heavy 3-ounce custard cups—the upright, porcelain kind—and don't open the oven door during the baking. You'll need to allow the batter to sit for at least an hour before baking; you can make it the night before, refrigerate it, then allow it to come to room temperature if you prefer.

If you want moist popovers with crispy domes, bake them as described in the recipe; for a drier popover, bake them at 350° for 45 or 50 minutes, prick them with a knife, and let them bake for another 5 minutes.

2 cups sifted all-purpose flour
½ teaspoon salt
2 cups milk
2½ tablespoons unsalted butter, melted
4 eggs, lightly beaten

Mix the flour and salt in a bowl. Combine the milk and 2 tablespoons of the butter together, then pour the mixture into the eggs and stir well. Slowly add the wet ingredients to the dry, stirring until they are just blended. Cover the batter and allow it to rest for an hour.

When ready to bake, preheat the oven to 400° and paint the insides of a dozen 3-ounce ovenproof custard cups with the remaining melted butter. Place the cups on a baking sheet. Strain the batter into a pitcher, then pour it into the cups, filling them no fuller than ½ inch from the tops. Bake the popovers for about 40 minutes, or until puffed and golden brown. Turn out of the cups and serve immediately.

MAKES 10 TO 12 POPOVERS

Chocolate Pots de Crème

If you don't have a set of eight of the lidded porcelain pots au crème especially made for this dish, you can use about six custard cups fitted with lids made of aluminum foil.

½ pound high-quality dark or semisweet chocolate
  broken into small pieces
2 cups heavy cream
6 tablespoons sugar
2 eggs plus 3 yolks
2 tablespoons coffee-flavored liqueur, such as Kahlúa

Preheat the oven to 350° and set a pot of water to boil. Melt the chocolate in the cream in a heavy-bottomed saucepan over very low heat, stirring occasionally so that it doesn't scorch. Stir in the sugar. In a mixing bowl, whisk the eggs and yolks together until just blended, then pour in the chocolate mixture, stirring constantly until well blended. Stir in the liqueur. Fill the cups, pouring slowly and carefully, and removing any bubbles on the surface with a demitasse spoon. Place lids carefully on each cup and place them in a baking pan.

Pour the boiling water about three fourths of the way up the sides of the pots. Bake for about 20 minutes, never letting the water in the pan return to a boil. The custards are done when a silver knife inserted in the middle comes out clean. Cool, chill, and serve in the pots.

SERVES 6 TO 8

OPPOSITE: **An eighteenth-century English butler's desk holds a model of** *Anne*, **the ship that brought Oglethorpe and his colonists to America, and more of the owner's orchids.** LEFT: **A Limoges pots de crème set.**

Spring Luncheon at the John Stoddard House

ABOVE: **In the formal dining room.**
OPPOSITE: **In the herb garden.**

✛

Tomato Aspic with Shrimp Mayonnaise
Fettuccine with Fresh Herbs and Clams
Black Pepper Sally Lunn
Sweet Potato/Pecan Pie

✛

JOHN STODDARD was a champion of midcentury construction downtown, hiring New York architect John Norris to build Italianate offices on the waterfront, then a row of Greek Revival town houses on Chippewa Square. This Italianate home was begun before the Civil War, but not finished until 1867. Its front-facing gable and added double bay distinguish the wealthy planter's home from the rest of the row. With cast-iron lintels, wide bracketed eaves, and a handsome, massive doorway, the house remains one of Savannah's finest.

Though the home is filled with period pieces, an octagonal solarium off the kitchen overlooks the herb garden and provides a perfect setting for this spring luncheon. Serve a Pinot Grigio or Gavi with the pasta.

Tomato Aspic with Shrimp Mayonnaise

Tomato aspic is a harbinger of spring, a favored starter course throughout the South. Shrimp are often added to the aspic, but here it is served with a dollop of homemade mayonnaise flavored with a few cooked shrimp.

For the aspic

1/4 cup boiling water

1 tablespoon (1 envelope) unflavored gelatin

2 cups tomato juice, or 1 16-ounce can crushed tomatoes, pureed

1 celery rib, minced

1 to 2 teaspoons grated onion

1/2 teaspoon salt

1/8 teaspoon cayenne

1 1/2 tablespoons sherry vinegar

Lettuce leaves for garnish

For the mayonnaise

1/2 teaspoon dry mustard, or 1 teaspoon prepared

1/2 teaspoon salt

1 egg

1 cup peanut oil

1 tablespoon fresh lemon juice

Several cooked shrimp, peeled

To make the aspic, pour the boiling water over the gelatin in a mixing bowl and stir well so that all of the gelatin dissolves. Add the remaining ingredients except the lettuce and mix well. Rinse six 1/2-cup ramekins in cold water and fill them with the aspic. Refrigerate to set and chill. To unmold, dip in hot water for a few seconds and invert onto a bed of lettuce.

To make the mayonnaise, put the mustard, salt, and egg in a blender and blend for about 20 seconds. Add the oil very slowly, at first by droplets, continually blending until all of the oil has been bound with the egg mixture and the mayonnaise is thick and creamy. Scrape down the sides with a rubber spatula, add the lemon juice, and blend briefly. With the motor running, start adding cooked shrimp, one at a time, blending well after each shrimp is added. Continue adding shrimp until the desired flavor is reached. Store well capped and refrigerated for no more than 3 days.

Serve the aspic with a dollop of mayonnaise.

SERVES 6

ABOVE: **Tomato aspic and shrimp mayonnaise.**
OPPOSITE: **Fettuccine with fresh herbs and clams.**

Fettuccine with Fresh Herbs and Clams

Clams have been harvested in the vast salt marshes of the lowcountry since time immemorial, but most of the little-necks, the smallest grade, were shipped up north until recently, when the mariculture of clams became popular outside Charleston. The grit-free clams are still grown in our marshes, but are now widely available. This classic Italian dish is a favorite wherever clams and herbs are available.

Salt

1 pound dried fettuccine

³/₄ cup extra-virgin olive oil

16 garlic cloves, more or less to taste, minced

4 dozen littleneck clams

¹/₂ to ³/₄ cup loosely packed mixed fresh herb leaves of your
   choice, such as basil, parsley, oregano, and chives

2 tablespoons unsalted butter

Freshly ground black pepper

Bring a large pot of water to a rolling boil, add a little salt, and return to a boil. Cook the pasta in the water, uncovered, while you prepare the sauce.

In a very large sauté pan, heat the oil with the garlic over medium-high heat for a few minutes until the oil is permeated with the garlic flavor, but do not let the garlic brown. Add the clams, cover the pan, and cook until all the clams have steamed open, about 5 minutes. Discard any clams that do not open.

While the clams and pasta are cooking, chop the herbs together well. You should have at least ¹/₄ cup. When the clams have opened, remove the lid, add the herbs all at once, and stir well into the clams and oil. Allow about half of the liquid to evaporate, increase the heat, then whisk in the butter. Serve immediately over drained pasta. Pass the pepper.

SERVES 4

Black Pepper Sally Lunn

This old-fashioned bread is England's version of brioche. Savannah's Damon Fowler is a culinary historian, food writer, and architect who has helped restore the grand tradition of antebellum southern cuisine through his cooking classes and his incomparable *Classical Southern Cooking* (Crown, 1995). This variation on his classic Sally Lunn, with no sugar or baking powder, includes some black pepper to complement this savory luncheon. Start the recipe the night before, or early in the day, so that the dough has time to rise. I've made a dozen rolls from the dough this time, but you can cook the dough in a loaf pan, a Bundt or tubular cake pan, or in large muffin tins.

1 cup milk

¼ teaspoon active dry yeast

3 eggs

1¼ pounds (about 4 cups) unbleached all-purpose flour, plus flour for dusting

1 teaspoon salt

4 tablespoons unsalted butter (½ stick) at room temperature

Freshly ground black pepper

The night before, or 6 to 8 hours before you plan to serve it, scald the milk and let it cool slightly to about 90°.

Add the yeast and stir to dissolve. Break the eggs into a bowl and beat them lightly. Stir the milk and yeast into the eggs.

Mix the flour and salt well together in a large mixing bowl. With a large fork, work in the butter until it is evenly incorporated and there are no large lumps. Make a well in the center and pour in the milk and egg mixture. Mix well with the fork until the dough is smooth, then turn it out onto a lightly floured surface.

Knead the dough lightly for about 5 minutes, then gather it into a ball. Wipe out the bowl and return the dough to it. Cover with a damp towel or plastic wrap and set aside to rise, 4 to 6 hours or overnight.

When the dough has doubled, lightly punch it down and knead it again lightly for about 1 minute, working in the black pepper.

Lightly grease a baking sheet. Make a dozen rolls by cutting the dough in half, then cutting each half in half again. Divide the quarters in thirds and roll each piece into a ball on a lightly floured surface or in your hands. Place the rolls on the pan, cover with a damp towel, and set aside until they have doubled again, about 1 or 2 hours.

For a loaf, lightly grease and flour a loaf or Bundt pan. Dust the dough with flour, then roll it into a log that will fit into the pan. Place the dough down in the pan, cover with a damp towel, and allow to rise as for the rolls.

Position a rack in the lower third of the oven and preheat to 400°. Bake the Sally Lunn until the top is lightly golden and the crumb is cooked through, about 20 minutes for rolls or 30 minutes if you are making a loaf.

MAKES 12 ROLLS OR 1 LOAF

LEFT: **Black pepper Sally Lunn.**
OPPOSITE: **Sweet potato/pecan pie is served on Chinese export porcelain.**

Sweet Potato/ Pecan Pie

This spring luncheon utilizes the last of autumn's sweet potatoes and pecans, combining two of the South's favorite desserts into one. This pie is a classic sweet potato pie in a pecan crust with a pecan pie topping. To grind the pecans, use a food processor in short pulses, resting between the pulses so that the blades don't get hot and render the nuts oily.

For the dough

1 cup soft southern flour (see Sources) or cake flour

¼ cup pecans, evenly and finely ground (see above)

3 tablespoons sugar

Pinch of salt

6 tablespoons unsalted butter

1 egg

1 tablespoon milk

For the sweet potato filling

¾ cup light brown sugar

½ teaspoon salt

1 teaspoon cinnamon

½ teaspoon freshly ground nutmeg

2 tablespoons molasses

1½ cups baked, peeled, and mashed sweet potatoes

⅔ cup half-and-half

2 eggs

4 to 6 tablespoons sherry or bourbon to taste

For the pecan topping

2 tablespoons unsalted butter at room temperature

¼ cup sugar

1 tablespoon molasses

1 large egg

1 cup pecan halves

To make the dough, mix the flour, pecans, sugar, and salt in a mixing bowl, then cut in the butter with a pastry blender or 2 knives. Mix the egg and milk together well, then stir into the flour and butter mixture until the dough just holds together. Wrap in plastic wrap and refrigerate for 30 minutes.

Roll the dough out into a 10-inch circle, then gently lift it up over the rolling pin and place it into an 8-inch pie pan, folding the overhang back over itself, then press it into place, gently flaring it out slightly over the pan's edge. Roll the pin over the top to press off the excess, then press the edge out with the fingertips again. Chill the crust while preheating the oven to 450°.

To make the sweet potato filling, mix all of the ingredients together well.

To make the pecan topping, mix the butter, sugar, molasses, and egg together well. Add the pecans and stir in well.

Bake the crust "blind"—line the crust with parchment or wax paper, then fill it with beans, rice, corn, or pie weights—for 8 minutes, or until the dough has begun to crisp. Remove the paper with the weights, reduce the heat to 425°, and bake for another 8 minutes. Remove the crust from the oven and reduce the heat to 375°.

Fill the crust with the sweet potato filling, then top with the pecan mixture. Bake the pie for about 35 minutes, or until set and golden brown. Allow to cool and serve at room temperature.

SERVES 8

OPPOSITE: **The solarium set for the informal luncheon.** ABOVE LEFT: **An assortment of silver serving pieces.** ABOVE RIGHT: **A corner of the formal drawing room.** BELOW: **Dogs on the deck.** BOTTOM: **Clock in the hallway.** LEFT: **A Catesby print.**

Fall Luncheon at the Conrad Aiken House

✝

Cheese Straws

Real Southern Iced Tea

Oyster Sausages

South Georgia Chicken Pie

Spinach Salad with Benne Vinaigrette and Fried Okra Croutons

Apple Pecan Torte

✝

THOUGH BUILT for Oscar Dibble in 1855, this handsome house is better known as Conrad Aiken's birthplace. It is a typical antebellum Savannah town house, two stories over a raised basement with a high stoop and balcony embellished with wrought- and cast-iron balustrades and brackets. A graceful curving staircase in the large entrance hall belies the mournful heritage of the property: at age eleven, Aiken found the bodies of his parents, killed by his father in a murder-suicide. Returning to the city later in life, he moved into the house next door (also called the Conrad Aiken House) and wrote his autobiographical *Ushant*, filled with haunting passages of Savannah.

OPPOSITE: **Aiken's immortalized stoop.**
ABOVE: **A French frumeau mirror hangs over a William Kent table in the foyer.**

In *Ushant*, Aiken describes a typical Savannah two o'clock dinner, followed by a Madeira tasting. He would have approved of the current owners' exuberant decoration of the house as well as this delicious fall meal. Here cheese straws are served with a big, oaky California Chardonnay in the courtyard, then iced tea is offered with the meal of oyster sausages, chicken pie, and spinach salad. A glass of Madeira would indeed be a fitting follow-up to the apple and nut torte that is served for dessert.

Cheese Straws

This is a classic lowcountry cocktail wafer, spicy with red pepper. They will keep for about a week in airtight tins and much longer well wrapped and frozen.

4 tablespoons (½ stick) unsalted
   butter, softened
½ pound sharp cheddar cheese,
   grated
¼ teaspoon salt
⅛ teaspoon ground cayenne
⅛ teaspoon crushed red pepper
⅞ cup all-purpose flour

Preheat the oven to 350°. Cream the butter with the cheese, then work in the seasonings and the flour with a large spoon or your hands.

   Roll the dough out thin and cut into strips about ½ inch wide and 6 to 8 inches long. Place the strips on a baking sheet and bake for about 25 minutes, or until golden. Remove to racks to cool.

MAKES ABOUT 4 DOZEN

Real Southern Iced Tea

The only tea grown in America is found about twenty miles south of Charleston on Wadmalaw Island at the Charleston Tea Plantation. Most southerners drink sweet tea by the gallon. When properly made, it's truly delicious and absolutely thirst-quenching. For an authentic flavor, use Charleston tea (see Sources) or at least an orange pekoe tea. Because tea does not improve with age, Charleston's is the freshest on the market. Orange pekoe tea is made with only the top two newest leaves on the bush, which is a member of the camellia genus.

   Always start with clean, nonreactive containers and cold water. Use one bag or one teaspoon of loose tea per glass. Pour boiling water over the tea and allow it to steep, covered, for 5 minutes, or until the tea is the desired strength. Most southerners put a little sugar in their tea while it is steeping, but you can sweeten it to taste afterward as well. Serve with lemon wedges and, if desired, freshly picked mint. Pour over ice in large glasses.

OPPOSITE: **Prize whippets have rule of the house,** TOP. **In the master bedroom,** BOTTOM. ABOVE: **Cheese straws are served with wine in the courtyard.** LEFT: **Tea is served from a fine Chinese export cider jug.**

Oyster Sausages

These delicious appetizers are traditionally served with lemon wedges and toast points on a bed of lettuce. Better still is to make Italian-style *bruschetta*, brushing baguette slices with olive oil and drying them in a low oven until they are crisp. You needn't have a meat grinder to make these sausages. Simply buy some bulk (country) sausage and season it to your own liking.

¼ pound sausage meat
½ cup fresh shucked oysters, chopped
1 egg yolk
2 tablespoons dry bread crumbs
Salt, freshly ground black pepper, and cayenne
Fresh or dried herbs of your choice to taste
3 to 4 tablespoons vegetable oil or clarified butter for frying
Lettuce leaves, lemon wedges, and toast points for garnish

Mix the sausage with the oysters in a bowl, then add the egg yolk and bread crumbs. Season to taste, then pinch off a little piece of the sausage and fry in a dry pan. Taste and correct the seasoning to suit your own palate.

Place a thin film of oil or clarified butter in a skillet and place over medium-high heat. Fry the sausages until golden brown all over, about 2 minutes on each side. Serve immediately on a bed of lettuce with lemon wedges and toast points.

SERVES 6

OPPOSITE: **Iced tea and oyster sausages begin this fall luncheon. The china cabinet is the owner's design.** LEFT: **In the entrance hall.**

South Georgia Chicken Pie

One of the current owners of the Aiken house hails from Americus, Georgia; so does this version of chicken pie. The old-fashioned chicken-in-milk-gravy filling and a simple biscuit top is southern comfort food at its finest.

For the stock and filling

1 small fresh chicken weighing about 3 pounds
1½ quarts water
2 large celery ribs, trimmed but left whole
1 medium onion, unpeeled but quartered
1 carrot, broken into pieces
1 bay leaf
Several sprigs of fresh herbs of your choice, to include some thyme

For the biscuit topping

2 cups sifted soft southern flour (see Sources), plus a little for dusting
2 teaspoons baking powder
1 teaspoon salt
5 tablespoons unsalted butter or lard
½ cup milk

For the filling and final assembly

4 tablespoons (½ stick) unsalted butter
3 tablespoons all-purpose flour
½ cup milk
1½ cups finely chopped onion (about 1 large)
Salt and freshly ground black pepper
2 hard-cooked eggs, chopped
2 tablespoons melted butter or cream

To make the stock and filling, discard any excess fat from the chicken cavity. Rinse the chicken well, then place in a stockpot with the water. Add the celery, onion, carrot, and herbs to the pot, bring it to a boil, and immediately reduce the heat to a simmer. Cook, skimming the pot frequently, until the meat is thoroughly cooked, about 1 hour.

Remove the chicken and the celery ribs from the pot and cool. Strain the rest of the solids out of the pot and discard. Refrigerate the strained stock. Remove the skin from the chicken and discard, then pull the meat from the bones and chop into uniform pieces. Discard any fat and the bones. Chop the cooked celery into small pieces, then set the chopped chicken and celery aside.

To make the biscuit topping, sift the dry ingredients

into a bowl, then cut in the butter with a pastry blender or 2 knives until it is evenly incorporated. Working swiftly, fold in the milk a little at a time with a rubber spatula until it is just blended in.

Dust a counter with some flour and scoop up the dough onto the dusted area. Place your fingers down into the flour to coat them, then *lightly* work the dough, using only your fingertips, until it is evenly blended. Roll or pat it out about ¼ inch thick into the shape of the 2-quart casserole you will be using for the pie. Cover with a damp tea towel while you make the filling.

To make the filling, preheat the oven to 425°. In a deep sauté pan over medium-high heat, melt the butter, then add the flour, stirring constantly until you have a smooth paste. Gradually stir in 2 cups of the reserved stock and the milk and continue cooking until the mixture is the consistency of thick cream, about 5 to 10 minutes. Remove from the heat. Add the onion, the chicken, and the celery to the mixture, stir well to combine, and taste for salt and pepper. Turn out into a 2-quart baking dish.

Scatter the eggs over the mixture, then top with the biscuit dough. Brush with melted butter or cream, then bake for about 15 minutes. If the biscuits aren't browned, you can run them under the broiler for a moment. Serve hot.
SERVES 6

ABOVE: **A group of objects on the English library table in the drawing room.** OPPOSITE: **Chicken pie and spinach salad.**

Spinach Salad with Benne Vinaigrette and Fried Okra Croutons

Spinach is one of the most common fall and winter crops on the Sea Island truck farms of the lowcountry. The dressing for this salad is flavored with garlic, lemon, and toasted benne; the fried okra topping is a last farewell to the foods of summer. If you can't find perfectly blemish-free okra, use frozen.

The corn flour is a very fine grind of cornmeal. If you can't find it, pulse some cornmeal to a finer grind in a blender.

For the fried okra
½ pound fresh okra, or 1 10-ounce package frozen cut-up okra
Peanut oil for frying
½ cup corn flour (see Sources)
Salt, freshly ground black pepper, and cayenne

For the salad and dressing
1 pound fresh young spinach leaves
2 tablespoons benne (sesame seeds), roasted (see page 39)
¼ cup fresh lemon juice
⅔ cup extra-virgin olive oil
1 garlic clove, minced
Salt and freshly ground black pepper

To make the okra, trim the stem ends from the okra pods and discard. Slice the pods into ½-inch pieces, then put them in a bowl of ice water for about 30 minutes. If using frozen okra, open the package and place in a colander to thaw.

Pour 2 or 3 inches of oil in a stockpot or Dutch oven over medium-high heat. While the oil is heating, drain the okra well. If the frozen okra isn't thawed, run water over it and gently separate the pieces.

In a shallow bowl, season the corn flour to taste with the salt, pepper, and cayenne. Line a colander with crumpled paper towels.

When the oil has reached 370°, dust the okra well in the corn flour and fry in the hot oil until golden, about 3 minutes. Maintain the temperature of the oil, don't crowd the pot, and drain the okra in the prepared colander before serving.

To make the salad, pick the spinach over, discarding any tough stems or yellowed leaves. Wash it well and dry thoroughly. Chill until serving.

For the vinaigrette, combine the remaining ingredients well just before serving. Allow diners to dress their own salad and garnish it with fried okra.

SERVES 6

Apple Pecan Torte

This is my version of Charleston's famous cake with the misnomer "Huguenot Torte." Regardless of its heritage, it's a delicious and simple way to end a fall meal with the flavorful new crops of crisp mountain apples and local pecans.

1 cup pecans, plus 8 perfect pecan halves
1 large, firm apple, peeled, cored, and cut up
2 eggs at room temperature
1 egg yolk at room temperature
7/8 cup sugar, plus a little more for the pecans
3/8 cup all-purpose flour
1/2 cup heavy cream

Lightly grease a 9-inch round cake pan, line it with wax paper or parchment, grease the paper, and lightly dust with flour.

Preheat the oven to 375° and put a pan of water in the bottom of the oven.

Finely grind 1 cup of pecans in a food processor, working in quick bursts so as not to render the nuts oily. Remove the nuts from the work bowl and add the apple pieces. Chop by pulsing quickly until the apple is uniformly, finely chopped.

Warm the bowl of an electric mixer, then beat the eggs and yolk on high speed until doubled in volume, about 10 minutes. Slowly add the sugar and continue beating until tripled in volume. The eggs should be very thick and lightly colored.

Sift the flour over the egg mixture, sprinkle the ground nuts all around, then the apples. Fold the mixture together gently but rapidly, making sure that you get all the ingredients off the bottom of the bowl mixed thoroughly into the mixture. Pour the batter into the pan and bake in the middle of the oven for about 25 or 30 minutes until the top is golden brown and the sides have begun to pull away. Don't push on the meringuelike top or it may cave in.

Place on a rack in a draft-free place and allow the cake to cool completely in the pan.

Lightly toast the perfect pecan halves in a skillet or oven, then, while they are hot, dip them in water, then roll them in sugar until lightly coated. Let them dry on a rack or paper towel.

When the cake is perfectly cool, invert it gently, remove the paper liner and discard, then turn the cake back over again onto a serving plate so that the crusty surface is on top again.

Whip the cream stiff and place 8 dollops of the cream around the cake. Garnish each dollop with a sugared nut and serve immediately.

SERVES 8

OPPOSITE: **In the upstairs drawing room.** ABOVE: **Apple pecan torte.**

OKRA

RIGHT: **Okra is trimmed down to, but not into, the pods.**

LEFT: **An okra plant blooms and fruits daily for months.** ABOVE: **Okra for sale from the bed of a pickup.**

OKRA APPEARS IN this collection steamed atop butterbeans, fried as croutons for a salad, featured in a soup, and pickled and set out as an hors d'oeuvre or even to replace the olives in a martini. Quintessentially lowcountry, okra — or gumbo — was brought directly from West Africa with the slave trade. Its pale yellow hibiscus flower brightens fields from May through November, and it grows so fast that every morning for months the grower can pick tender young pods no longer than a little finger. It is one of the most flavorful of vegetables, tasting slightly of the sea. Its mucilaginous qualities are legend, but it can be cooked so that it's not slimy at all:

Buy okra no longer than your finger. The pods should all be the same size and bright green, with no blemishes or hard spines. If you don't spend time meticulously choosing fresh okra, you may as well buy frozen, which was picked at a perfect stage of ripeness; it will be better than inferior fresh. Trim the stems down to, but not into, the pods so that they remain whole in cooking. Place them in a saucepan with just a little bit of water, cover tightly, and cook at a boiling temperature, so that the okra steams, until it is just done, about 10 minutes.

Early Supper at the Adam Short House

ABOVE: **The facade of the house.**
OPPOSITE: **The dining room set for supper. The miniatures are family portraits; the dinnerware is English Masons ironstone.**

✦

Pickled Okra Martinis
Sausage Biscuits
Marinated Top Round
Pole Beans and New Potatoes
Bread Pudding with Whiskey Sauce

✦

O NE OF TWO adjoining buildings built by Adam Short in 1853, this house on Calhoun Square follows the typical mid-century pattern of two stories, three bays wide, over a raised basement, with a high stoop at one of the end bays. Short was a bricklayer who built the houses on specu-lation. Calhoun Square was one of the last of James Oglethorpe's 1733 plan to be formed. The Short houses sold quickly—and twice—in a matter of months.

The current owners have restored the carriage house and planted the courtyard with exotic and native flora. "Nothing was bought for the house," the owner says of his eccentric collection of eighteenth-, nineteenth-, and twentieth-century art and furnishings. The print of Oglethorpe on the desk is a mid-nineteenth-century engraving of the

original made by Samuel Ireland on February 18, 1785. Oglethorpe is shown reading, without spectacles, a book he had purchased at the auction of the library of Dr. Johnson. The sketch was once used to adorn paper currency issued by the Bank of Augusta in 1836 and by the State of Georgia in 1862.

This spring supper begins with martinis made with pickled okra (see Condiments) and sausage biscuits, followed by a quick and simple variation on meat and potatoes, with the first pole beans of the season. A big red from the Rhône valley is the ideal wine for this. Dessert is a classic southern bread pudding with whiskey sauce.

ABOVE: **Seventeenth-century-style triangular, or three-square, chair.** LEFT: **Pickled okra martinis and sausage biscuits are served on a reproduction Savannah Granada server.** OPPOSITE: **An eighteenth-century English secretary is topped with a nineteenth-century bookcase inherited by the owner.**

Pickled Okra Martinis

Okra pickles (see Condiments) are set out on the sideboard alongside the sausage biscuits. Guests nibble them as I make otherwise traditional martinis with chilled vodka or gin, a splash of vermouth, and a garnish of pickled okra.

Sausage Biscuits

These cheesy crackers are favored treats at southern parties. They're easy to make and will keep for a week in airtight containers.

½ pound bulk (country) sausage, preferably hot (spicy)
6 tablespoons (¾ stick) unsalted butter at room temperature
1 cup grated extra-sharp cheddar cheese
¾ cup all-purpose flour
½ teaspoon salt
Perfect pecan halves (optional)

Fry the sausage in a skillet over medium-high heat until it is rendered of fat. Drain and allow to cool.

Cream the butter and cheese together, then sift the flour and salt together over the cheese mixture, stirring well to combine. Crumble the sausage and mix it into the dough with your hands. Chill for about 30 minutes.

Preheat the oven to 350°. Pinch off small pieces of the dough and roll them into 1-inch balls. Place the balls about an inch apart on a baking sheet, then flatten each ball, using a pecan half if desired. Bake for 15 to 20 minutes, or until they brown. Serve warm or at room temperature.

MAKES ABOUT 5 DOZEN

Marinated Top Round

The top round is a delicious cut of beef that is sometimes marketed as London broil; it's less expensive than flank steak and equally delicious. The marinade is really just some olive oil seasoned with fresh herbs and garlic; it keeps the meat from drying out when grilling or broiling. You can add a splash of red wine to the marinade if you wish, but don't add lemon juice because it can break down the meat.

This makes more than enough for four people, but the meat is delicious left over and cold as well. If you want to grill the meat, simply cook it over a medium fire for about five minutes per side, basting frequently with the marinade.

1 top round steak (about 2 pounds)
1/4 cup dry red wine (optional)
A few drops of a bottled hot sauce
2 garlic cloves, minced
2 tablespoons chopped parsley
2 tablespoons chopped fresh marjoram or oregano
  and thyme
1/2 cup olive oil
Salt and freshly ground black pepper

Place the meat in a large sealable plastic bag. Put the wine, hot sauce, garlic, and herbs in a small bowl and whisk in the oil. Add the salt and pepper, then pour the marinade over the meat. Squeeze out any air in the bag, seal it, and make sure the meat is well coated with the marinade. Refrigerate overnight or leave at room temperature for an hour.

When ready to cook, preheat the broiler and place the meat in a baking dish. Pour the marinade over it, then broil the meat about 6 inches from the element for about 5 minutes per side. Let the meat rest for 5 minutes after it is cooked, then cut into thin slices across the grain on the bias.
MAKES 6 TO 8 SERVINGS

Pole Beans and New Potatoes

When the first of the pole beans and new potatoes hit the markets in the spring, this dish appears in both fancy city and country homes throughout the lowcountry. Try to find tender beans without a heavy string, such as Kentucky Wonders, and do not overcook them. The small amount of water may be surprising, but the recipe works perfectly well.

2 pounds pole beans
2 pounds small new potatoes
1 smoked ham hock, about 1/2 pound
1/3 cup water

String the beans, leaving the tender young tip intact. Clean the potatoes and cut them in half. Put the beans in the bottom of a heavy saucepan that has a tight-fitting lid. Add the potatoes, hock, and water. Simmer, covered, until the potatoes are done, 30 to 45 minutes. Serve hot.
SERVES 4 TO 6

ABOVE: **Marinated top round with pole beans and new potatoes.** OPPOSITE: **Caladium and akebia.**

Bread Pudding with Whiskey Sauce

This southern classic can be made ahead and reheated or served cold, warm, or hot from the oven. The buttery whiskey sauce should be warm.

¼ cup raisins
¼ cup bourbon, plus a little more if needed
¼ pound (1 stick) unsalted butter, melted
4 cups French bread torn into bite-size pieces (from a baguette weighing about ½ pound)
2½ cups milk
1 small cinnamon stick
½ teaspoon pure vanilla extract
4 eggs
1 cup sugar

Soak the raisins in the bourbon for at least 30 minutes or overnight if possible.

Preheat the oven to 350° and brush the insides of a 1½-quart soufflé dish with some of the butter.

Put the bread in a large mixing bowl. Drain the raisins, reserving the bourbon, and add to the bread. Place the milk, cinnamon, and vanilla in a saucepan and cook over medium heat until scalded (bubbles just begin to break the surface). Beat 3 of the eggs with ½ cup of sugar until well blended, then gradually stir in the scalded milk. Pour the mixture over the bread and raisins and discard the cinnamon stick. Allow to soak while you prepare the whiskey sauce.

Whisk the remaining egg and sugar together in a bowl set over simmering water until very light and nearly doubled in size. Whisk in the melted butter a little at a time, then whisk in the reserved bourbon (if you don't have ¼ cup, add enough to make up for what was absorbed by the raisins). Leave the sauce over the water, but remove it from the stove.

Place the greased soufflé dish inside a larger roasting pan. Add the bread mixture to the greased pan, then pour hot water into the roasting pan to a depth of about 1 inch. Place in the oven and bake for about 45 minutes, or until a knife inserted in the center comes out clean. Drizzle whiskey sauce over the pudding as it is served.

MAKES ABOUT 6 SERVINGS

LEFT: **Bread pudding with whiskey sauce.** TOP: **Passionflower.**
ABOVE: **An espaliered *Parrotia persica* in the courtyard.**

Grilled Fish on a Dock at Isle of Hope

✦

Benne Wafers

Crudités with Sweet Potato Dip

Grilled Dolphin and Green Tomatoes

Mango Relish

Hoppin' John Salad

Strawberry Ice Cream and Angel Food Cake

✦

OPPOSITE: **Docks on the river.**
ABOVE: **Bamboo utensils float if they fall overboard.**

ONE OF THE lowcountry's most beautiful suburbs, Isle of Hope is a charming tidewater village on a high bluff overlooking the Skidaway River. Originally built as summer retreats for wealthy neighboring plantation squires, several of the homes along the scenic bluff were constructed in the nineteenth century. As both Savannah and the village grew, the houses became permanent residents of water-loving "sandlappers," as residents of the lowcountry are known. Most of the homes along Bluff Drive have long docks that jut out into the marsh-lined river. Nearly everyone is a fisherman of sorts.

When fish are running, it's not unusual to invite neighbors over for

grilled fish on the dock. Dolphin is today's catch. One of the most beautiful fish, dolphin flush with brilliant yellows, blues, and emeraldlike greens when they are excited. The colors quickly fade, but the large-flaked, sweet white flesh is among the most delicious of seafoods.

Because so many tourists in the lowcountry think that dolphin on a menu means "Flipper," many restaurants have the annoying habit of calling dolphin "mahi-mahi," which is the Hawaiian name of a Pacific form of the fish. Sandlappers know better; I've brushed it with a little olive oil and grilled it with green tomatoes. The salad is a variation on hoppin' john, the traditional New Year's good luck dish. Bright mango relish complements the fish, and for dessert there's homemade strawberry ice cream and angel food cake. For wine, try a Vinho Verde or Sauvignon Blanc.

LEFT: **Houses along the bluff in Isle of Hope feature sweeping porches in a variety of styles.**

Benne Wafers

Benne wafers are of two types in the lowcountry—sweet and salty. These savory ones are spiced with hot pepper. Serve them with drinks before dinner.

1⅓ cups all-purpose flour
¾ teaspoon salt
⅛ teaspoon cayenne
¼ pound (1 stick) unsalted butter, cut into pieces
3 tablespoons ice water
⅔ cup roasted sesame seeds (see page 39)

Preheat the oven to 300°. Sift the flour, salt, and cayenne together into a mixing bowl, then cut in the butter with a pastry blender or 2 knives until it is evenly incorporated and there are no large lumps. Gradually add the ice water until the dough just holds together, then add the sesame seeds and push the dough together into a ball.

Roll the dough out very thin and cut into small wafers with a small cookie or biscuit cutter, lifting them onto a baking sheet with a metal spatula. Bake for about 30 minutes, flipping them over when they are about halfway done. Store in airtight tins.
MAKES 2 TO 3 DOZEN

Crudités with Sweet Potato Dip

Serve this dip with crudités and watch how surprised your guests are by the intriguing flavor.

1 pound sweet potatoes (about 1 large or 2 small)
1 whole head garlic
2 to 4 tablespoons extra-virgin olive oil
2 tablespoons fresh lemon juice
Salt and bottled hot pepper sauce

Place the sweet potatoes and garlic head in a baking dish, drizzle with a little oil, and bake at 375° until they give to the touch, about 45 minutes.

Peel the sweet potatoes and place the baked flesh in the work bowl of a food processor. Cut the base off the garlic head and squeeze the roasted flesh out into the sweet potatoes. Puree the mixture, adding the oil, lemon juice, and salt and hot pepper sauce to taste, until the mixture has a good consistency for a dip. Serve at room temperature.
MAKES ABOUT 2 CUPS

ABOVE: **Crudités, sweet potato dip, benne wafers, and pickled okra.**

Grilled Dolphin and Green Tomatoes

If you can't find dolphin or mahimahi, use another firm, white-fleshed fish. This recipe is simplicity itself.

2 pounds firm green tomatoes
Salt and freshly ground black pepper
¼ cup, or more, olive oil
6 dolphin fillets, about 1 inch thick (about ½ pound each)

Build a charcoal fire or set a gas grill to medium to pre-heat. Slice the tomatoes, discarding the stem end, and place the slices in a shallow container such as a rectangular glass casserole dish. Season them with salt and pepper, then drizzle the oil over them and turn until they are lightly coated.

When the fire is ready, pick up each slice of tomato with tongs, allowing any excess oil to drip back into the container. Place the slices on the grill and cook until black grill marks appear and the slices are thoroughly warmed through, about 4 minutes on each side. In the meantime, place the fish down in the oil and turn, making sure each piece is well coated. Add more oil, salt, and pepper, if needed. Remove the tomato slices to a serving platter, then place the fish on the grill. Cover the grill and place the serving platter of tomatoes on top to stay warm. Cook the fish for 5 mintues on the first side, uncover the grill, turn the fish, and cook uncovered until the flesh just flakes when pried with a fork, about another 5 minutes. Serve immediately.
SERVES 6

Mango Relish

Mangoes have been imported into lowcountry ports since the early eighteenth century. This brightly flavored salsa will keep for a couple of days in the refrigerator but is best when made at the last moment. It takes just a few minutes to make it.

2 mangoes, peeled, pitted, and diced
1 orange, peeled, seeded, sectioned, and cut up
1 cup chopped scallions, whites and some of the green
1 fresh hot pepper such as a jalapeño, seeded and minced
½ cup chopped red bell pepper
¼ cup fresh lime juice
Salt
¼ cup fresh cilantro leaves

Combine the mangoes, orange, scallions, peppers, and lime juice and toss well. Season to taste with salt. Toss in the cilantro just before serving.
SERVES 6

LEFT: **Mango relish complements the rice salad and the grilled foods.**

Hoppin' John Salad

Hoppin' john, my namesake, becomes a salad in this version. In the lowcountry, the traditional bean for the dish is the cowpea, or dried field pea; more than three hundred varieties are grown. Throughout most of the South, though, the widely available blackeyed pea is used. You can use fresh or frozen peas, but don't cook them with any seasoning.

1½ cups cooked and drained blackeyed peas
2¼ cups cooked long-grain white rice
¼ cup chopped red onion
¼ cup chopped celery
½ red bell pepper, seeded and chopped
½ hot pepper such as a jalapeño, seeded and minced
¼ cup loosely packed fresh mint
¼ cup loosely packed fresh parsley or chervil
1 garlic clove, peeled
Fresh lemon juice from 1 or 2 lemons
3 tablespoons extra-virgin olive oil
Salt and freshly ground black pepper

Toss the peas, rice, onion, celery, and peppers together in a large mixing bowl. Place the herbs and garlic on a cutting board and chop together finely. Add to the peas and rice mixture and toss. Add a tablespoon of lemon juice to the oil and whisk together, then pour over the salad, tossing well. Correct the seasoning with lemon juice, salt, and pepper.

SERVES 6

Strawberry Ice Cream

Strawberries are the first fruits of the year; their season marks the beginning of good deep-sea fishing. The ice cream is custard based, rich with egg yolks and cream. The egg whites go into angel food cake, quite simply the easiest cake to make.

You can cook the custard, prepare the strawberries, and bake the cake the day before. Bring the churn to the cookout and make everyone take a turn—it only takes 20 minutes to freeze, and it can sit in the ice until serving time.

For the strawberries
2 pints strawberries
1 tablespoon red wine vinegar
1 tablespoon sugar

Hull the berries and cut them in half; quarter the larger ones. Place them in a nonreactive container and sprinkle with the vinegar and sugar. Toss, cover well, and refrigerate until ready to churn the ice cream.

For the ice cream
1 vanilla bean
1 quart milk
12 egg yolks
1½ cups sugar
1 pint whipping cream

Scrape the seeds from the vanilla bean into the milk. Add the pod to the milk and scald in a heavy saucepan, then remove from the heat. In another large, heavy-bottomed saucepan, mix the yolks well with the sugar. Strain the scalded milk into the egg mixture gradually, stirring constantly. Discard the vanilla bean. Cook the custard over medium-low heat, stirring constantly, until it coats the back of a spoon, about 10 minutes. Allow to cool, then refrigerate.

When the custard is thoroughly chilled, add the cream and the berries to it in a churn and freeze according to the manufacturer's instructions.

MAKES ½ GALLON, ABOUT 12 SERVINGS

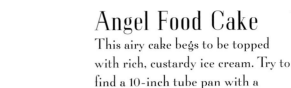

Angel Food Cake

This airy cake begs to be topped with rich, custardy ice cream. Try to find a 10-inch tube pan with a removable bottom; it allows you to remove the cake.

1 cup sifted soft southern flour (see Sources) or cake flour
1½ cups sugar
12 egg whites at room temperature
¼ teaspoon salt
1 teaspoon cream of tartar
1 teaspoon vanilla extract

Preheat the oven to 375°. Sift the flour with ½ cup sugar at least three times and set aside.

In the large bowl of an electric mixer, beat the egg whites, salt, cream of tartar, and vanilla on the medium speed until the whites turn opaque. Increase the speed to high and gradually add the remaining cup of sugar, mixing until all of the sugar is beat in and the whites hold firm peaks. Sift a fourth of the flour at a time into the whites and fold in gently but thoroughly until all of the flour is folded in.

Gently turn the batter out into a perfectly clean and dry 10-inch tube pan and smooth the top. Bake for about 30 minutes, or until a straw inserted into the cake comes out clean. If the center tube is taller than the pan, invert the cake for an hour to cool. If the pan has no extension, place the inverted pan over the neck of a bottle to cool.

To remove the cake, slip a thin knife between the cake and the pan all around the outer edge and the tube. Invert the cake on a platter and lift off the pan. Don't cut the cake, but use 2 forks with their tines back to back to pull the cake apart in opposite directions. Serve with ice cream.

SERVES 10 TO 12

ABOVE: **Strawberry ice cream and angel food cake.** OPPOSITE: **Shutters block the afternoon sun.**

PEPPERS

IMAGINE A WORLD without tomatoes, potatoes, or corn; without chocolate, sweet potatoes, or pecans. Incomprehensible? That's precisely what Europe and Asia were before Columbus's discovery of America. What's more, it was a world addicted to exotic seasonings and spices, to black pepper and cinnamon and cloves. You could even say that taste was responsible for that auspicious voyage: Columbus was searching for a shorter route to the Spice Islands.

Perhaps even more astounding is that it was also a world without the capsicum peppers — the bells and jalapeños and cayennes and a hundred others that spice the cooking of the Mediterranean, of Africa, of India, of China, and of Southeast Asia. Columbus took hot peppers back to Spain on his maiden voyage, and Mediterranean cooking was changed forever. By 1643, the French had founded Cayenne in Guyana, naming their outpost after the Tupi Indian word for hot pepper. More important for the lowcountry, slaves were traded along the same routes as spices. The West Africans who were brought to the lowcountry as slaves in the seventeenth and eighteenth centuries were long used to a cuisine highly spiced with the capsicums. It was the hand of the black cook that spiced the foods of the English, French, and German settlers here. Our cooking is creole, like that of Louisiana, but it has more African influences.

At the root of our cooking is an almost instinctual response to the foods being cooked. Salting, timing, and seasoning can be done entirely through the nose of a real lowcountry cook. Geechees, the local descendants of slaves, say "She has an old hand" of the cook who needn't taste the pepper to know how hot it is. She may not necessarily have raised it from seeds taken from last year's crop, but she knows by the mingling smells in the pot just how much to add.

Peppers are so revered that they are grown as cash crops on the barrier islands, on balconies of downtown mansions, in the yards of beach houses, and wherever in the lowcountry that there's a little sun. The bells are grown far from the hot peppers; capsicums are wildly promiscuous and cross-pollination is common. We put them in slaw and relishes and in soups and stews. They are as common as tomatoes and perhaps even more popular.

BELOW: **Baskets of peppers ready to go to market.**

LEFT: **An assort-ment of pepper vinegars.**

Condiments

PICKLES AND PRESERVES, RELISHES AND chutneys—these are the real hallmark of southern cooking. They reflect both the practicality of country cooks and the sophisticated palates of the residents of the port cities. The slave and spice trades forever traversed the same routes; with the ships came Indian chutneys and teas, exotic plants from the Orient, and fruits from the Caribbean.

Most traditional recipes were meant as a way of preserving foods. You need not make the large quantities called for in the older recipes; and if you plan to refrigerate the preserves and use them within a few weeks, there's no need to process them in a boiling water bath. If you do plan to store them for any length of time, or you're giving them as gifts, process them according to the following instructions:

Always begin with new metal lids for screw-on lids and new rubber rings for clamping lids. Sterilize all of your equipment by placing it in a boiling water bath. Fill the jars to within a half inch of the tops, then run a thin spatula or chopstick down inside each jar to release any air bubbles. Wipe the top of the jar clean with a clean cloth. Place the metal lids or rubber rings on the jars, then fasten the lids. Turn the filled jars upside down once to ensure a proper seal, then place them carefully down in a water bath, covering the jars by at least 1 inch of water. Process, or allow to boil, for the amount of time called for in each recipe. If a metal lid does not seal by being sucked down by a vacuum, store the jar in the refrigerator and use the contents within a few weeks. Always remove pickles and preserves from their jars with clean instruments; fingers and buttered knives will encourage bacterial growth that will spoil your efforts.

LEFT: **An array of lowcountry pickles and preserves set on a counter overlooking a Charleston piazza.**

Pickled Shrimp

These aren't really condiments, but they are "put up" more often than the old traditional relishes and chutneys. If you put pickled shrimp out at a party, they'll disappear before you know it. Many lowcountry gardens are filled with old Roman laurels— bay trees—brought back from the ever-traveling planter-merchant elite, many of them avid gardeners. Don't scrimp on the quantity of bay leaves or the quality of olive oil: they're each essential for flavor. Make these at least twenty-four hours in advance of serving. They'll last for two weeks refrigerated.

1½ quarts water
¼ cup crab or shrimp boil, such as
   Old Bay Seasoning
2 pounds small to medium shrimp
   (about 50 per pound)
1 tablespoon salt
1 cup extra-virgin olive oil
⅓ cup fresh lemon juice
1 teaspoon mustard seeds
1 teaspoon celery seeds
2 garlic cloves, minced
25 to 30 bay leaves
1 medium onion, thinly sliced

In a large pot, bring the water to a boil. Have a bowl of ice cubes ready. Add the shrimp boil to the boiling water, drop the shrimp into the pot, and cook until the shrimp are just done—no more than 3 minutes. Do not let the water return to a boil. Drain, then plunge the shrimp into ice to stop the cooking. Peel the shrimp when they're cool enough to handle and set aside.

Sterilize a quart jar in a pot of boiling water. Combine the salt, oil, lemon juice, mustard and celery seeds, and garlic and set aside. Place about 15 of the shrimp in the jar, then add a layer of about 4 bay leaves, then a layer of onion slices. Continue making layers until the jar is filled and all the ingredients are used. Pack the jar tightly, pushing down on the ingredients with a tall, narrow olive or capers jar if necessary.

When the jar is full, stir the oil mixture well and pour slowly into the jar. Use a spatula handle or a tool made for the purpose to run down the sides to release air bubbles and to make sure the jar fills. If well packed, the jar will hold all the ingredients perfectly. Put the lid on the jar and turn it over once to make sure everything is coated with oil and the air bubbles are out. Open the jar again and push down on the ingredients again so that they are covered with a film of oil.

Refrigerate for at least 24 hours before serving. Always use a clean fork to remove the shrimp, never a finger, and when returning the jar to the refrigerator, make sure the remaining ingredients are covered with a film of oil.
MAKES 1 QUART

ABOVE: **Pickled shrimp.**

Hot Pepper Vinegar

Hot pepper vinegar is always passed with cooked greens in the lowcountry. You can make it very simply by replacing a quarter of the vinegar in a bottle with hot peppers and setting aside for a week. Spiciness varies with peppers. The following recipe is just a little more trouble, but the resulting vinegar has nuances of flavor that make it worth the effort.

Mixed hot peppers, about 1 pound
1 garlic clove, peeled
3 cups white vinegar
3/4 cup water
2 tablespoons salt
1 small onion, peeled and chopped
1 1/2 teaspoons mustard seeds

Pack a sterilized quart jar with the mixed hot peppers, then add the garlic clove. Mix the remaining ingredients in a nonreactive pot and cook at a low boil for about 30 minutes, covered.

Pour the boiling liquid over the peppers, seal the jar, and process in a boiling water bath for 10 minutes.

MAKES 1 QUART

Pear Chutney

This is a perfect complement to salty country ham. In the lowcountry, it is made with the hard local Kieffer pears, but you can use any underripe pear. When there's leftover country ham, grind it with equal amounts of this chutney and put it out with crackers as an appetizer: ham paste always disappears when offered.

1 pound hard, underripe pears, peeled, seeded, and chopped
1 lightly packed cup light or dark brown sugar
1 cup apple cider vinegar
1 teaspoon mustard seeds
1/2 teaspoon cayenne
1/4 cup crystallized ginger, chopped
1/2 teaspoon ground cinnamon
1/2 teaspoon freshly ground white pepper
1/4 teaspoon freshly grated nutmeg
2/3 cup light or dark raisins or a mixture of the two
2/3 cup chopped onion
1 tablespoon fresh lemon juice

Cook the pears in water to cover until they are medium-soft. Drain, saving the water, then make a syrup of the water and the brown sugar by boiling in a nonreactive pot until thick, about 20 to 30 minutes.

Add the pears and the remaining ingredients to the pot and cook for another 30 minutes, or until the raisins are soft, the onions are clear, and the chutney is thick.

The chutney will keep in the refrigerator for months.

MAKES ABOUT 3 1/2 CUPS

Pear Relish

Our hard local Kieffer pears—a cross between the common and Oriental pear—also find their way into this relish that is served with beans and rice or with roast meats, such as the oven-roasted pork with rosemary on page 84. Peel, core, and cut the pears into chunks, then use a food processor to grind the fruit.

1 peck (about 10 pounds) Kieffer or hard, underripe pears, peeled, cored, and coarsely chopped
5 medium onions, peeled and cut into eighths
3 red bell peppers, seeded, stemmed, and quartered
3 green bell peppers, seeded, stemmed, and quartered
2 fresh red cayenne or jalapeño peppers, seeded and stemmed
1 tablespoon mustard seeds
1 teaspoon cloves, preferably freshly ground (1 tablespoon whole cloves)
1 tablespoon cinnamon, preferably freshly ground (3 sticks)
1 tablespoon ground turmeric
3 cups sugar
1 quart white vinegar
1 tablespoon salt

Mix the pears, onions, peppers, and spices in a bowl, then grind them in batches in a food processor until uniformly chopped. Add them to the sugar, vinegar, and salt in a nonreactive pot and boil, stirring often, for about an hour, or until thickened.

Pour the relish into sterilized jars and seal. Process for 20 minutes in a boiling water bath.

MAKES ABOUT 9 PINTS

Pickled Okra

These are the favorite lowcountry pickle, possibly because they are time-consuming to make: you must pack the okra pods tightly in the jars, alternating one up and one down so as to fill the jar and to prevent them from floating to the top. Use only freshly picked, bright green, blemish-free okra, no more than finger-long. Each pound of okra will yield two pints of pickles. You can multiply this recipe with no problem.

1 pound small young okr1711a pods, all the same size
4 garlic cloves, peeled
2 hot peppers
1 teaspoon mustard seeds
1 cup water
1 heaping tablespoon salt
2 cups white vinegar

Wash the okra and trim the stems a little, but not down into the pod. Pack the okra tightly in 2 sterilized wide-mouthed pint jars, alternating stems up and stems down. Divide the garlic, peppers, and mustard between the jars.

Bring the water, salt, and vinegar to a boil, then pour it over the okra to within $1/2$ inch of the rims. Place a lid and ring on each jar, lower the jars in a water bath, and process at a full boil for 10 minutes.

Remove the jars from the bath and allow to cool completely. If the lids have not sealed, refrigerate the pickles. Store the pickles for 2 months, then chill before serving.

MAKES 2 PINTS

Dilly Beans

In warm years, you can grow green beans in the lowcountry for ten months. Try to use very fresh, young beans for this recipe. Taste the beans, and if they feel furry in the mouth, blanch them for a moment or two before beginning. This pickle is very easy to make.

3 pounds tender young green beans, trimmed at
    the stem end
6 garlic cloves, peeled
6 flowerheads of fresh dill
$3^{3}/_{4}$ cups white vinegar
$3^{3}/_{4}$ cups water
$3/_{8}$ cup salt
$1^{1}/_{2}$ teaspoons crushed red pepper

Pack the beans into 6 sterilized pint jars, then add a garlic clove and a flowerhead of dill to each jar. Combine the remaining ingredients in a nonreactive saucepan, bring to a boil, then pour into each jar to within $1/_{4}$ inch of the rims. Run a plastic spatula handle or a chopstick around the inside of each jar to release air bubbles. Add the lids and seal. Process in a boiling water bath for 10 minutes.

Allow the pickles to cure for at least 2 weeks, then chill well before serving.

MAKES 6 PINTS

Spiced Peaches

Pickled peaches are a staple of the holiday table in the lowcountry. Some of the funniest moments of my childhood were when the spicy globes would slide from under someone's fork and go bouncing across the table, rolling precariously toward a wineglass. They are served with salty country ham and with turkey, in lieu of the New Englander's cranberry sauce.

Use a large $1^{1}/_{2}$-liter clamp lid jar for this recipe (there are several French brands widely available), then serve it during one of the big holiday meals. You won't need to process this recipe in a boiling water bath.

3 pounds (8 to 14 small to medium) firm ripe peaches
    with no blemishes
8 to 14 whole cloves
1 cup white vinegar
$2^{1}/_{3}$ cups sugar
1 cinnamon stick
A 2-inch piece of crystallized ginger

Drop the peaches a few at a time into boiling water, removing them with a slotted spoon after about a minute. Plunge them into cold water. Peel them; the skins should slip right off. Stick a whole clove into each peach.

Bring the remaining ingredients to a boil in a nonreactive saucepan and add the peaches. Cook uncovered at a low boil until they are tender but not falling apart, about 20 minutes. Place the peaches down in a $1^{1}/_{2}$-liter wide-mouthed jar, pour in the liquid, and push the cinnamon stick and ginger down among the peaches. Seal the jar and store in a cool, dark, and dry place until the holiday season.

MAKES $1^{1}/_{2}$ LITERS

Sources

I'VE ALWAYS MAINTAINED THAT THE finest foods are fresh and local, but it's true that you can't make lowcountry food without real grits any more than you can make Southeast Asian cuisine without real fish sauce. I do believe, however, that if you can't find any honest-to-goodness country ham then you can use some prosciutto and at least capture the style if not the very essence of the recipe that calls for it. Common sense and integrity are intertwined in the kitchen.

For the adventurous among you or for those of you who have tasted real southern ingredients and want the real thing, here is a list of sources for some of our finer specialty foods.

Bland Farms Vidalia Onions
P.O. Box 506, Glennville, GA 30427; phone (800) VIDALIA
The world-renowned sweet onions.

✦

Carolina Bay Trading Company
P.O. Box 13405, Charleston, SC 29422; phone (803) 406-1300
Palmetto Food Focus is the newsletter of this food distributor specializing in products grown and produced in South Carolina. Call for a recent copy or for a list of purveyors in your area.

✦

Charleston Tea Plantation
6617 Maybank Highway, Wadmalaw Island, SC 29487; phone (800) 443-5987
The only tea grown in America. Delicious because it is fresh; tea does not improve with age.

✦

Crosby's Seafood
2019C Cherry Hill Lane, Charleston, SC 29405; phone (803) 577-3531

The bright orange roe of the female Atlantic blue crab is the distinguishing flavor of our famous she-crab soup. Crosby's will ship it and other local delicacies such as shad roe and soft-shell crabs via air freight.

✦

Hoppin' John's
30 Pinckney Street, Charleston, SC 29401; phone (803) 577-6404
My culinary bookstore offers a wide range of books about food. We also ship a variety of southern foods such as Carolina Gold rice, country hams, our own brand of whole-grain, stone-ground corn products—grits, cornmeal, and corn flour—and condiments such as dilly beans, pear chutney, and green tomato relish.

✦

Limehouse Produce
616A Wappoo Road, Charleston, SC 29407; phone (803) 556-3400
The Limehouses will ship green tomatoes and green peanuts in season via air freight. No credit cards.

✦

LowCountry Exotic Mushroom Farm
P.O. Box 867, John's Island, SC 29457; phone (803) 559-9200
Owner Ben Cramer grows several varieties; if your local grocer doesn't carry shiitakes or oyster mushrooms or portobellos, call Ben.

✦

Manchester Farms
P.O. Box 97, Dalzell, SC 29040; phone (800) 845-0421
Quail has been raised for the restaurant and retail trade for twenty-five years in this small South Carolina town. Call to locate a grocer or mail-order business in your area that carries the delicious birds.

✦

Palmetto Pigeon Plant
P.O. Drawer 3060, Sumter, SC 29151; phone (803) 775-1204
Since 1923, squab (young pigeon) has been raised on whole grains and pure springwater at Palmetto. Poussin and pheasant are also available, via air freight. Call for a distributor or grocer in your area.

✦

Planters Three
P.O. Box 92, Wadmalaw Island, SC 29412; phone (800) 772-6732
Another sweet onion grown on a barrier island just south of Charleston.

✦

White Lily Foods
P.O. Box 871, Knoxville, TN 37901; phone (423) 546-5511
White Lily produces soft southern flour from winter wheat. With little gluten, it's needed for southern biscuit and cake recipes. Call for a distributor or grocer in your area.

Index

Adam Short House, 150–57
Aiken, Conrad, 117, 118, 139, 140
Alligator Pear and Crabmeat Salad, 114
Ambrosia, 33
Angel Food Cake, 165
Apple Pecan Torte, 147
Ardsley Park, 122–29
Asparagus, fresh, 102
Aspic, tomato, 132
Avocado, stuffed with crabmeat, 114

Baked Orange Custard with Cranberry Glaze, 96–97
Barley and Wild Rice, 106
Beans. See specific types
Beaufort, South Carolina, 10, 13, 61–115
Beef broth, 39
Beets, oven-roasted, 85
Benjamin Phillips House, 37–43
Benne
    green bean salad with, 39
    vinaigrette, 145
Benne Wafers, 162
Best Lemonade, 72
Beverages
    Creole café au lait, 33
    lemonade, 72
    martinis with pickled okra, 153
    real southern iced tea, 141
Biscuits
    ham, 31
    sausage, 153
Blackeyed Pea Cakes with Roasted Pepper Puree, 55
Blackeyed peas, hoppin' John salad, 164
Black Pepper Sally Lunn, 134
Blake, John, 20
Blue Cheese and Pecan Wafers, 125
Boiled Peanuts, 72
Bouillon, tomato, 111
Bread Pudding with Whiskey Sauce, 156
Breads
    black pepper Sally Lunn, 134
    cornbread, 40
    icebox rolls, 111
    pita, 74
    popovers, 129
    sweet potato corn muffins, 56
    See also Biscuits; Wafers

Briggs, Loutrel, 53
Broth, beef, 39
Butter Beans and Okra, 26

Café au lait, creole, 33
Cakes and cookies
    angel food cake, 165
    apple pecan torte, 147
    Greek cookies, 106
    lemon squares, 45
    red velvet cake, 77
    sweet potato cake, 51
Carrots, oven-roasted, 85
Catfish, fried, 25
Chaplin, Thomas B., 66
Charleston, South Carolina, 10, 15–59
Charleston Tea Plantation, 141
Cheese
    in sausage biscuits, 153
    wafers, 125
Cheese Straws, 141
Chicken pie, South Georgia, 144
Chocolate Pots de Crème, 129
Chutney, pear, 171
Clams, fettuccine with fresh herbs and, 133
Cobbler, peach, 114–15
Coffee, creole café au lait, 33
Cold Curried Squash Soup, 22–23
Cole Slaw, 75
Condiments, 169–72
    hot pepper vinegar, 171
    mango relish, 163
    pear chutney, 171
    pear relish, 84, 171
    pickled shrimp, 170
    shrimp mayonnaise, 132
Conrad Aiken House, 139–47
Consommé, shrimp, 90
Cookies. See Cakes and cookies
Corn, in frogmore stew, 72
Cornbread, 40
Corn muffins, sweet potato, 56
Crab, 78–79
    salad with alligator pear, 114
    she-crab soup, 48
Cranberry glaze, 96
Cream Gravy, 32–33
Crème fraîche, 86
Creole, shrimp, 56
Creole Café au Lait, 33
Croquettes, potato, 93
Croutons, fried okra, 145

Crudités with Sweet Potato Dip, 162
Custard. See Puddings and custards

Desserts
    angel food cake, 165
    apple pecan torte, 147
    baked orange custard with cranberry glaze, 96
    bread pudding with whiskey sauce, 156
    chocolate pots de crème, 129
    Greek cookies, 106
    lemon squares, 43
    peach cobbler, 114–15
    persimmon pudding, 86
    plum tart, 27
    red velvet cake, 77
    scuppernong pie, 76
    strawberry ice cream, 164
    sweet potato cake, 51
    sweet potato/pecan pie, 135
Dibble, Oscar, 139
Dilly Beans, 172
Dolphin, 161
    grilled with green tomatoes, 163

Eggplant, fried, 49
Elizabeth Barnwell Gough House, 88–97

Fettuccine with Fresh Herbs and Clams, 133
Fish
    fried catfish, 25
    grilled dolphin, 163
    poached with ginger and lemon thyme, 83
    See also Shellfish
Fowler, Damon, 134
Fried Catfish, 25
Fried Eggplant, 49
Frogmore Stew, 72
Fruit. See specific fruits
Fuller, Thomas, 80

Gibbes, William, 52–53
Ginger, poached fish with, 83
Glaze, cranberry, 96
Grapes, scuppernong pie, 76
Gravy, cream, 32–33
Greek Cookies, 106
Green Bean and Benne Salad, 39
Green beans, dilly pickled, 172

Greens, turnip, 93
Grilled Dolphin and Green Tomatoes, 163
Grits, 32–33
Gumbo. See Okra

Halidon Hill, 28–35
Ham, country, 32–33
Ham Biscuits, 31
Hess, Karen, 83
Hoppin' John Salad, 164
Hors d'oeuvres. See Snacks and hors d'oeuvres
Hot Pepper Vinegar, 171
Huguenin, Mary, 28

Icebox Rolls, 111
Ice cream, strawberry, 164
Iced tea, 141
Ireland, Samuel, 152
Isle of Hope, 159–65

Jay, William, 117
John Blake House, 20–27
John Stoddard House, 130–37

Lamb, rack of, 102
Lemonade, 72
Lemon Squares, 43
Locke, John, 15

Mahi-mahi, 161, 163
Mango Relish, 163
Marinated Top Round, 154
Martinis, pickled okra, 153
Mashed Sweet and White Potatoes with Garlic Chives, 127
Maxcy, Milton, 108
Mayonnaise, shrimp, 132
Meat
    braised rabbit in white wine, 91
    marinated top round, 154
    rack of lamb, 102
    sautéed veal chops, 125
    slow-roasted pork, 84
    See also Poultry
Meyer lemons, 45
Microwaving, fresh asparagus, 102
Muffins. See Breads
Mushroom types, 125

Norris, John, 130

Oglethorpe, James, 150, 152
Okra, 148–49
    butter beans and, 26
    buying and cooking tips, 149
    fried croutons of, 145
    pickled, 153, 172
Okra Soup with Steamed Rice, 39
Orange
    in ambrosia salad, 33
    and cranberry glaze, 96
    in Greek cookies, 106
Orange pekoe tea, 141
Oven-Roasted Beets and Carrots with Fresh Mint, 85
Oyster mushrooms, 125
Oysters, 78–79
    Rockefeller turnovers, 100
Oyster Sausages, 143

Pan-Fried Quail with Grits, Country Ham, and Cream Gravy, 32–33
Peach Cobbler, 114–15
Peaches, spiced, 172
Peanuts, boiled, 72
Pear Chutney, 171
Pear Relish, 84, 171
Pears Poached in Champagne, 59
Pecan
    apple torte, 147
    and blue cheese wafers, 125
    sweet potato pie, 135
Pepper(s), 166–67
    hot, 171
    puree of roasted, 55
Persimmon Pudding, 86
Phillips, Benjamin, 37
Pickled Okra, 172
Pickled Okra Martinis, 153
Pickled Shrimp, 170
Pickles, 172
Pies and tarts
    chicken pie, 144
    plum tart, 27
    scuppernong pie, 76
    sweet potato/pecan pie, 135
Pilau, 26
Pinckney, Roger, 28
Pita Bread, 74
Plum Tart, 27
Poached Fish with Ginger and Lemon Thyme, 83
Pole Beans and New Potatoes, 154
Popovers, 129
Pork, slow-roasted with rosemary and pear relish, 84
Potato Croquettes, 93
Potatoes
    mashed, 127
    pole beans and, 154
    See also Sweet Potato headings
Pots de crème, chocolate, 129

Poultry
    chicken pie, 144
    pan-fried quail, 32–33
    roasted squab, 49
Puddings and custards
    baked orange custard with cranberry glaze, 96
    bread pudding with whiskey sauce, 156
    chocolate pots de crème, 129
    persimmon pudding, 86

Quail, pan-fried, 32–33

Rabbit Braised in White Wine with Tomatoes, 91
Rack of Lamb, 102
Real Southern Iced Tea, 141
Red pepper puree, 55
Red Rice, 26
Red Velvet Cake, 77
Relish. See Condiments
Rhett, Edmund, 108
Rhett, Robert, 110
Rice, 12, 15, 44
    and barley, 106
    cooking method, 44
    okra soup with steamed, 39
    tomato pilau, 26
Riverview, 98–107
Roasted Red Pepper Puree, 55
Roast squab, 49
Rockefeller Turnovers, 100
Roebling, Cornelia, 52–53
Rolls, icebox, 111
Rosemary, pork slow-roasted with, 84

Salads
    ambrosia, 33
    cole slaw, 75
    crabmeat and alligator pear, 114
    green bean and benne, 39
    hoppin' John, 164
    spinach with benne vinaigrette, 145
Sally Lunn, 154
Salsa, mango, 163
Sauce, whiskey, 156
Sausage
    in frogmore stew, 72
    oyster, 143
Sausage Biscuits, 153
Sautéed Veal Chops with Oyster Mushrooms, 125
Savannah, Georgia, 10, 12, 116–67
Scalloped Turnips, 85
Scuppernong Pie, 76
Secession House, 64, 108–15
Seigneur, Vincent le, 46
Sesame seeds. See Benne
She-Crab Soup, 48

Shellfish, 78–79
    clams with fettuccine, 133
    frogmore stew, 72
    oyster sausages, 143
    pickled shrimp, 170
    Rockefeller turnovers, 100
    she-crab soup, 48
    shrimp consommé, 90
    shrimp creole, 56
    shrimp mayonnaise, 132
    See also Fish
Short, Adam, 150
Shrimp, 78–79
    in frogmore stew, 72
    pickled, 170
Shrimp Consommé, 90
Shrimp Creole, 56
Shrimp Mayonnaise, 132
Slow-Roast Rosemary Pork with Pear Relish, 84
Snacks and hors d'oeuvres
    benne wafers, 162
    boiled peanuts, 72
    cheese straws, 141
    crudités with sweet potato dip, 162
    sausage biscuits, 153
Soups
    cold curried squash, 22–23
    okra with steamed rice, 39
    she-crab, 48
    shrimp consommé, 90
    tomato bouillon, 111
Sources, mail-order, 173
South Georgia Chicken Pie, 144
Spiced Peaches, 172
Spinach, wilted, 127
Spinach Salad with Benne Vinaigrette and Fried Okra Croutons, 145
Squab, roast, 49
Squash, cold curried soup, 22–23
Stew, Frogmore, 72

Stoddard, John, 130
Strawberry Ice Cream, 164
Sweet Potato Cake, 51
Sweet Potato Corn Muffins, 56
Sweet Potato Dip, 162
Sweet potatoes, mashed with white potatoes and garlic chives, 127
Sweet Potato/Pecan Pie, 135

Tabby Manse, 80–87
Tarts. See Pies and tarts
Tea, iced, 141
Tomato Aspic with Shrimp Mayonnaise, 132
Tomato Bouillon, 111
Tomatoes
    green, grilled with dolphin, 163
    rabbit braised in white wine with, 91
    in red rice, 26
Tombee Plantation, 66–77
Turnip Greens, 93
Turnips, scalloped, 85
Turnovers, Rockefeller, 100

Veal chops, sautéed with oyster mushrooms, 125
Vegetables. See specific kinds
Vinaigrette, benne, 145
Vincent le Seigneur House, 46–51
Vinegar, hot pepper, 171

Wafers
    benne, 162
    cheese straws, 141
    pecan and blue cheese, 125
Whiskey Sauce, 156
Wild rice, barley with, 106
William Gibbes House, 52–59
Wilted Spinach, 127

Conversion Chart
Equivalent Imperial and Metric Measurements

American cooks use standard containers, the 8-ounce cup and a tablespoon that takes exactly 16 level fillings to fill that cup level. Measuring by cup makes it very difficult to give weight equivalents, as a cup of densely packed butter will weigh considerably more than a cup of flour. The easiest way therefore to deal with cup measurements in recipes is to take the amount by volume rather than by weight. Thus the equation reads:

1 cup = 240 ml = 8 fl. oz.   ½ cup = 120 ml = 4 fl. oz.

It is possible to buy a set of American cup measures in major stores around the world.

In the States, butter is often measured in sticks. One stick is the equivalent of 8 tablespoons. One tablespoon of butter is therefore the equivalent to ½ ounce/15 grams.

LIQUID MEASURES

Fluid Ounces	U.S.	Imperial	Milliliters
	1 teaspoon	1 teaspoon	5
¼	2 teaspoons	1 dessertspoon	10
½	1 tablespoon	1 tablespoon	14
1	2 tablespoons	2 tablespoons	28
2	¼ cup	4 tablespoons	56
4	½ cup		110
5		¼ pint or 1 gill	140
6	¾ cup		170
8	1 cup		225
9			250, ¼ liter
10	1¼ cups	½ pint	280
12	1½ cups		340
15		¾ pint	420
16	2 cups		450
18	2¼ cups		500, ½ liter
20	2½ cups	1 pint	560
24	3 cups		675
25		1¼ pints	700
27	3½ cups		750
30	3¾ cups	1½ pints	840
32	4 cups or 1 quart		900
35		1¾ pints	980
36	4½ cups		1000, 1 liter
40	5 cups	2 pints or 1 quart	1120

SOLID MEASURES

U.S. and Imperial Measures		Metric Measures	
Ounces	Pounds	Grams	Kilos
1		28	
2		56	
3½		100	
4	¼	112	
5		140	
6		168	
8	½	225	
9		250	¼
12	¾	340	
16	1	450	
18		500	½
20	1¼	560	
24	1½	675	
27		750	¾
28	1¾	780	
32	2	900	
36	2¼	1000	1
40	2½	1100	
48	3	1350	
54		1500	1½

OVEN TEMPERATURE EQUIVALENTS

Fahrenheit	Celsius	Gas Mark	Description
225	110	¼	Cool
250	130	½	
275	140	1	Very Slow
300	150	2	
325	170	3	Slow
350	180	4	Moderate
375	190	5	
400	200	6	Moderately Hot
425	220	7	Fairly Hot
450	230	8	Hot
475	240	9	Very Hot
500	250	10	Extremely Hot

Any broiling recipes can be used with the grill of the oven, but beware of high-temperature grills.

EQUIVALENTS FOR INGREDIENTS

all-purpose flour—plain flour
coarse salt—kitchen salt
cornstarch—cornflour
eggplant—aubergine

half and half—12% fat milk
heavy cream—double cream
light cream—single cream
lima beans—broad beans

scallion—spring onion
unbleached flour—strong, white flour
zest—rind
zucchini—courgettes or marrow